Becoming a Holy Spirit-Led, Manifest Child of God Who Ignites Unstoppable, Joyful, Revival Fires of Supernatural Power

REVIVAL FIRE-STARTERS BOOK 1

Fullness of Joy

THAT ONLY COMES WITH SALVATION

JOHN W. NICHOLS

THAT ONLY COMES WITH SALVATION

Becoming a Holy Spirit-Led, Manifest Child of God Who Ignites Unstoppable, Joyful, Revival Fires of Supernatural Power

JOHN W. NICHOLS

God and You and Me
CREATIONS

Fullness of Joy that Only Comes with Salvation:
Becoming a Holy Spirit-Led, Manifest Child of God,
Who Ignites Unstoppable, Joyful, Revival Fires of Supernatural Power
Copyright © 2024 by John W. Nichols.
All rights reserved. Printed in the United States of America. No part of this book may be used or reproduced in any manner whatsoever without written permission except in the case of brief quotations embodied in critical articles or reviews.
Published in Shenandoah, Texas, by God and You and Me CREATIONS.
For information contact: John@GodAndYouAndMe.com

Edited by Joanne Hillman, www.JoanneHillman.com
Cover design and book formatting by John Nichols
www.GodAndYouAndMe.com/BookHelp

Cover Photo, Brooklyn Font, and Breathine Font downloaded from CreativeFabrica.com with permission by the Subscription License

Scripture quotations marked AMP are taken from the Amplified® Bible, Copyright © 2015 by The Lockman Foundation. Used by permission. www.Lockman.org

Scripture quotations marked AMPC are taken from the Amplified® Bible, Copyright © 1954, 1958, 1962, 1964, 1965, 1987 by The Lockman Foundation. Used by permission. www.Lockman.org

Scripture quotations marked NASB are taken from the NEW AMERICAN STANDARD BIBLE®, Copyright © 1960,1962,1963,1968,1971,1972,1973,1975,1977,1995 by The Lockman Foundation. Used by permission.

Scripture quotations marked NKJV are taken from the New King James Version®. Copyright © 1982 by Thomas Nelson. Used by permission. All rights reserved.

Scripture quotations marked NLT are taken from the Holy Bible, New Living Translation, copyright © 1996, 2004, 2015 by Tyndale House Foundation. Used by permission of Tyndale House Publishers, Inc., Carol Stream, Illinois 60188. All rights reserved.

Scripture quotations marked TPT are from The Passion Translation®. Copyright © 2017, 2018 by Passion & Fire Ministries, Inc. Used by permission. All rights reserved. ThePassionTranslation.com.

Translations of Hebrew and Greek words taken from Strong's Exhaustive Concordance, Copyright © 1890 by James Strong, S.T.D., LL.D. Public Domain.

Print Edition January 2024 ISBN: 978-1-7328093-3-8
Epub Edition January 2024 ISBN: 979-8-8691-1609-3
Kindle Edition January 2024 ASIN: B0CSF6NDGS
10 9 8 7 6 5 4 3 2 1

For the Church,
the body and the bride of Christ.

Contents

Introduction 1

Ch. 1: The State of Our Broken World 11

Ch. 2: The Joy of Salvation 21

Ch. 3: The Temple and the Sacrifice 29

Ch. 4: Living as a Child of God and Joint-Heir with Christ 37

Ch. 5: You Are More Like Christ than Fallen Adam 45

Ch. 6: Experiencing the Fullness of Joy 55

Ch. 7: Being a Person of Faith, Hope, and Love 63

Ch. 8: Understanding Water Baptism 71

Ch. 9: The Wonder of Being a New Creation and Ambassador of God 81

Ch. 10: The Freedom that Comes from Laying Down Your Life 91

Ch. 11: What It Looks Like to Bear God's Fruit 101

Ch. 12: The Joy of Abiding in Christ 109

Additional Notes 119

Free Stuff! 123

References 125

About the Author 127

Introduction

And this gospel of the kingdom will be preached in all the world as a witness to all the nations, and then the end will come.

Matthew 24:14 NKJV

I WROTE THIS BOOK for passionate Holy Ghost fire-starters who desire to be a part of the great end-time harvest. Are you one of them? I don't know about you, but I am not waiting in a bunker for Jesus to come rescue me from the coming antichrist. I want to be counted among the Spirit-led sons and daughters of God, which the entire world is waiting to be revealed (Romans 8:19).

The salvation found in Jesus Christ of Nazareth was not only meant to be Hell-fire Insurance. God planned for us to carry on what Jesus started with this race we are running. When Jesus ascended after conquering sin and the grave, I believe He was passing the baton to His many brethren (Romans 8:29). But how well is the Church carrying that baton and running the race Jesus and His apostles did?

Fullness of Joy

> *And you know that God anointed Jesus of Nazareth with the Holy Spirit and with power. Then Jesus went around doing good and healing all who were oppressed by the devil, for God was with Him.*
>
> Acts 10:38 NLT

Surely you have read, recorded from the very mouth of our Savior, that we are destined for even greater works than He (John 14:12). This series of books is meant to equip our generation for those greater works. I consider each book a general lesson in discipleship with many keys, hidden gems, and revelations from scripture you may have never heard emphasized in this way.

The idea is that you would become a Holy Spirit-led manifest child of God, who ignites unstoppable, joyful, revival fires of supernatural power! Yes, I know that's a mouthful, and it barely describes what I am trying to say. Let me briefly break it down. My goal is that you would:

- listen to and obey the Holy Spirit
- represent God and His glory as His child
- carry the fire of God into your family, community, workplace, school, and wherever you go.

These Holy Ghost fires will spread, and no one can put them out. They are fires which are full of joy, fires that draw people to desire God (where they experience Him, and they don't want to leave His presence), and fires of supernatural power to bring deliverance, healing, restoration, and transformation!

But you may wonder who I am... When I was about 19 years old in the year 2000, I was in deep depression, unquenchable anger, and addiction to drugs, sex, and alcohol when God suddenly revealed His love for me and radically transformed my life. I had the Word, but I didn't know the power of God, so I continued to limp along, fighting my addictions, but totally in love with Jesus. I married my wonderful wife, Trinna, in 2006 and we struggled to live the Christian life together until shortly after we had our second daughter in 2014, and God shook my world by calling me into ministry. You can read more about these testimonies in my other books: God is Here and Healing is Here.

Ever since that moment, Trinna and I have pursued the call He has placed on our lives. It has led our family to serve in churches, prisons, communities, and nations. In 2016, we began a two-year focus on local missions through an apartment ministry. Then in 2018, God called us to take the gospel into a foreign land, and He spoke Rome to Trinna and without her saying a word, He confirmed it to me through a series of visions. We spent the next four years being prepared, refined, and shaped into who God needed us to be in Rome. We learned about the need for God's holy fire to purify and how we can overcome the strongholds in our lives. We learned about ministering by the power of the Holy Spirit, the reality of spiritual warfare, and people's need for deliverance and Jesus to heal their hearts. And we learned how to share the gospel boldly on the street, how to really "do church," and make disciples who would multiply.

The great commission tells us to, "Go... and make disciples of all the nations, baptizing them in the name of the Father and the Son and the Holy Spirit, teaching them to observe all that I (Jesus) commanded you..." (Matt. 28:19-20 NASB). We must go to others, not only ask them to come with us to church. We need to accept our responsibility to disciple people in the ways of Jesus, and train them to train (disciple) others who will also obey what He has commanded. This is how the church grows and every believer can be a part of this eternal change. We believe God has called all of us to help people see how He loves them, chooses them, transforms them, and has a purpose for their lives.

In 2022, my family moved to Italy as missionaries. We believe God has been brewing something here, and the pot is about to boil and overflow. We can hear the sound of revival coming on the wind. Rome has never seen revival the way other parts of the world have. It is a very spiritually dark place, but the darkness is nothing compared to the light of God, and we believe we are on the cusp of Him moving in power here. Not only that, we believe God is about to pour out His glory like never before all over the earth. But is the Church ready?

> *But [the time is coming when] the earth shall*
> *be filled*
> *With the knowledge of the glory of the*
> *LORD,*
> *As the waters cover the sea.*
> Habakkuk 2:14 AMP

This is why I am writing this series, to do my part in helping people get ready for the next great move of God. In this first book, we are going to lay the groundwork of our identity as children of God and—if we allow this truth transform us—we will have joy. We'll be talking about:

- The state of our broken world: what God intended, what the enemy did, and what is our part

- What it really means to be saved

- The temple and the sacrifice

- Living as a child of God and joint-heir with Christ

- How you are more like Christ than fallen Adam

- Experiencing the fullness of joy

- Being a person of faith, hope, and love

Fullness of Joy

- Understanding water baptism
- The wonder of being a new creation and ambassador of God
- The freedom that comes from laying down your life
- What it looks like to bear God's fruit
- The joy of abiding in Christ

We'll continue our series in several more books and we will dive deep into subjects like:

- Becoming supernatural by worshiping in spirit and in truth
- Breaking all the boxes, by falling in love with the God of the Bible, and not religion
- All-consuming fire leading to transformation and sanctification
- Gathering with the Spirit-led glorious bride
- More real realms are found in the Spirit
- Changing the world by being a freedom fighting miracle worker
- Becoming an uninhibited child of God
- Being a revival glory carrier in evangelism and discipleship

- Prospering for the kingdom and becoming a blessed blessing

Peter replied, "Repent and return to God, and each one of you must be baptized in the name of Jesus, the Anointed One, to have your sins removed. Then you may take hold of the gift of the Holy Spirit. For God's promise of the Holy Spirit is for you and your families, for those yet to be born and for everyone whom the Lord our God calls to himself."

Peter preached to them and warned them with these words: "Be rescued from the wayward and perverse culture of this world!"

Those who believed the word that day numbered three thousand. They were all baptized and added to the church.

Every believer was faithfully devoted to following the teachings of the apostles. Their hearts were mutually linked to one another, sharing communion and coming together regularly for prayer. A deep sense of holy awe swept over everyone, and the apostles performed many miraculous signs and wonders. All the believers were in fellowship

Fullness of Joy

as one body, and they shared with one another whatever they had. Out of generosity they even sold their assets to distribute the proceeds to those who were in need among them. Daily they met together in the temple courts and in one another's homes to celebrate communion. They shared meals together with joyful hearts and tender humility. They were continually filled with praises to God, enjoying the favor of all the people. And the Lord kept adding to their number daily those who were coming to life.

Acts 2:38-47 TPT

Is there any reason we can't live out the above passage of the Bible today? My goal with these books is to inspire us to experience even more!

This Free Download Will Help Set You Ablaze!

You'll get the most out of this book by using the accompanying workbook, which you can get either free as a printable PDF (or to view on your phone/tablet), or by buying the print edition on Amazon. This workbook includes thought provoking questions, journaling prompts, and practical next steps suggestions.

In the download, I'll also include other free resources that you can take advantage of (listed below)! If you want to purchase the perfect bound print edition, use this link: GodAndYouAndMe.com/recommends/fullness-of-joy-workbook/

Free Stuff!

| Fullness of Joy Workbook | Simple Steps to Hearing God | Walk with God, Change the World | Revolutionize Your Quiet Time |

Subscribe at: GodAndYouAndMe.com/joy-free-stuff

Get All These Free Resources Together

- Printable PDF of the *Fullness of Joy that Only Comes with Salvation Workbook.* (also viewable on phone/tablet).
- *God is Trying to Tell You Something.* An audio teaching in MP3 format, focused on the key to hearing God, common ways God speaks, and

practical steps to hear Him today.
- *7 Keys to a Successful Time of Devotion to God.* A PDF with steps to include in your quiet time.
- *Navigating the Maze of Life with God.* A 60-page PDF about giving your life to God, being filled with the Holy Spirit, and walking in the power of the Holy Spirit to live the life God intended you to live.
- Additional content only available to subscribers on GodAndYouAndMe.com. You can unsubscribe at any time and I promise not to spam you.

Get these free resources here (Most phones are capable of using the camera app to follow this link. Simply open the camera on your phone and point it at the page):

GodAndYouAndMe.com/joy-free-stuff

Chapter 1

The State of Our Broken World

WHEN WE TRULY AND deeply know who God is and who He created us to be, we will have no choice but to feel joy. But this treasure is locked away, hidden beneath shrouds of deception and lies of hopelessness. Hints rise to the surface as even the darkest human heart has an inexplicable desire for paradise. I don't mean relaxing on a beautiful island with all your needs attended to. Rather, God placed a hunger in us for perfect peace, perfect health, and perfect relationship with Him and each other.

Even though many can't say they've tasted this paradise, we all feel great dissatisfaction when we look at the world.

Fullness of Joy

Humanity inherently knows it's wrong to suffer the depravity and atrocities we face in our social constructs like poverty, slavery, and war. Even in nature we see diseases, animal attacks, and disasters like earthquakes and tsunamis, and we know this is not what we were made to experience. Why?

God Intended Something Beautiful

In the first chapter of the Bible, we see God create everything, step back from His masterpiece, and declare that it is very good. He even made the first humans in an intimately special way, and Scripture records something amazing:

> *So God created man in His own image; in the image of God He created him; male and female He created them. Then God blessed them, and God said to them, "Be fruitful and multiply; fill the earth and subdue it; have dominion over the fish of the sea, over the birds of the air, and over every living thing that moves on the earth."*
>
> Genesis 1:27-28 NKJV (see also Psalm 8:3-6)

In the Garden of Eden, Adam and Eve had that perfect

peace, perfect health, and perfect relationship with God and each other. They even had a great destiny and heavenly mandate, which we still carry today. That is to represent God to the earth.

The Bible only records one boundary that God gave mankind, "You may freely eat the fruit of every tree in the garden—except the tree of the knowledge of good and evil. If you eat its fruit, you are sure to die." (Genesis 2:16b-17 NLT) Even if you're not familiar with the story, you won't be surprised that only one chapter later man will face a temptation to break the rule God gave him.

But Something Got Twisted

In Genesis 3, we find a deceptive evil in the form of a serpent was also in the garden. Genesis doesn't tell us much about the serpent, called Satan, but Ezekiel 28:13-19 shows us he was originally an angelic being God intended to guard Eden and humanity. Through other verses scattered throughout Scripture, we find that this guardian cherub betrayed God because of pride and likely due to jealousy of mankind being created in God's image. Satan and other evil forces are at play still to this day, but our focus right now is on what happened to humanity in the garden.

The serpent said to the woman, "You surely

will not die! For God knows that in the day you eat from it your eyes will be opened, and you will be like God, knowing good and evil." When the woman saw that the tree was good for food, and that it was a delight to the eyes, and that the tree was desirable to make one wise, she took from its fruit and ate; and she gave also to her husband with her, and he ate.
Genesis 3:4-6 NASB

Jesus called the devil the father of lies (John 8:44), and this is the beginning of a pattern the enemy continues to follow every time the word of God is spoken. He comes behind the seed of God's word to destroy it, or at least keep it from bearing fruit in our lives (Mark 4:1-20). Everything the serpent said here in Genesis 3 was a twisting of the truth.

God told Adam that he would die if he ate this fruit, and though the body and soul lived on in a corrupted state, the spirit of mankind died. The father of lies promised our eyes would be opened, but this act closed our eyes to the spiritual realm. The serpent also said, "you will be like God," but God had already declared we were like Him. Lastly, Satan promised we would know good and evil, but in eating this fruit we became so intimately acquainted with good and evil—we can still barely discern the difference.

> *... you have become **dull in your [spiritual] hearing and sluggish [even slothful in achieving spiritual insight]**... discriminate and distinguish between **what is morally good and noble and what is evil**...*
>
> Hebrews 4:11; 14 AMPC
> (emphasis added)

Our Redemption and Purpose

From the beginning, God wanted humanity to walk in deep fellowship with Him, learning from Him as we represented Him and His kingdom on the earth. He wanted us to rely on Him to know the difference between good and evil. This is still His desire, but because of what happened in the garden, this truth was hidden by sin, lies, blindness, and death.

The Bible says that Adam's fallen sinful nature spread to all people (Romans 4:12), sin brings death (Romans 6:23), and that all have sinned (Romans 3:23). If we're honest we see this all around us including in ourselves. But God knew we would be trapped in this state, and He had a plan from the beginning to save us.

Jesus was God visiting us in human form; but He also showed us how we should live. He was obedient to His Heavenly Father even unto death. He lived without sin, yet took the penalty of our sin on the cross when He died. And

Fullness of Joy

in His resurrection, Jesus conquered sin and the grave. Now whoever believes that Jesus is the Son of God and confesses Him as Lord will be saved (Romans 10:9). And through His joyful obedience, many have come to God.

> ... let us strip off every weight that slows us down, especially the sin that so easily trips us up. And let us run with endurance the race God has set before us. We do this by keeping our eyes on Jesus, the champion who initiates and perfects our faith. Because of the **joy** awaiting him, he endured the cross, disregarding its shame. Now he is seated in the place of honor beside God's throne.
> Hebrews 12:1-2 NLT
> (emphasis added)

Jesus meant for us who follow Him to run the race He did. God destined us to represent heaven, to the point of laying down everything so we can join in His purposes for the earth. But we can have joy even as we take up our crosses and follow Jesus. We can strip off the sin and everything weighing us down, knowing that His way is better, and that He is going to work through our sacrifice in beautiful ways.

I pray for you to have a deeper revelation of God's intentions for mankind, and His plans for your life. A flood of the joy of the Lord will wash over you as you receive. If you are following Jesus and laying your life down for Him, is there still something keeping you from experiencing His joy? If you can see a need for your relationship with God to be rekindled or grow, don't be discouraged, or hear any lies of defeat. His mercies are new every morning and He will help you. Wherever you are, and especially if you haven't given your life to Him, pray the prayer below, recognizing what He has done for us and aligning yourself with His plans for the world.

Prayer

Father, thank You for creating the world good. Thank You for even making humanity in Your image and likeness. I recognize the enemy and mankind corrupted what You originally intended the world to look like. I recognize I too have sinned and there are ways the enemy has trapped me. I'm sorry for this, God, and how I have tried at times to live apart from You according to my own faulty, righteous standard. Thank You for making a way for me to be truly righteous through Jesus Christ's life, death, and resurrection. I declare that I believe Jesus is the Son of God. I believe

Fullness of Joy

> *He was the only one who lived a sinless life. I believe He died a sinner's death for all people, including me. Thank You, Jesus, for taking on my sin, and taking the punishment of death I deserved. I believe You didn't stay dead, Jesus, but the power of the Holy Spirit raised You to life. Right now, I submit myself to You, Jesus, as my Lord and my Savior. I want to run the race You intended me to run. God, please empower me to do this with Your Holy Spirit. Please remove every weight and sin from me. And please help me experience joy as I live the life You created me to live. In Jesus's name, amen.*

Don't Forget!

If you haven't already, you can download the free accompanying workbook to view on your phone/tablet or as a printable PDF. It will help you think deeper about these topics and apply the Biblical truths, especially if you step out in faith and follow the recommended Action Items. I created it as another tool for you to become a Holy Spirit-led, manifest child of God, who ignites unstoppable, joyful, revival fires of supernatural power!

Perfect-bound print edition also available for purchase on Amazon:

GodAndYouAndMe.com/recommends/fullness-of-joy-workbook

Get the workbook and other free resources here (Most phones are capable of using the camera app to follow this link. Simply open the camera on your phone and point it at the page):

GodAndYouAndMe.com/joy-free-stuff

Chapter 2

The Joy of Salvation

*"Make me hear **joy and gladness**, That the bones You have broken may rejoice. Hide Your face from my sins, And blot out all my iniquities. Create in me a clean heart, O God, And renew a steadfast spirit within me. Do not cast me away from Your presence, And do not take Your Holy Spirit from me. Restore to me the **joy of Your salvation**, And uphold me by Your generous Spirit. Then I will teach transgressors Your ways, And sinners shall be converted to You."*

Psalms 51:8-13 NKJV
(emphasis added)

THE WRITER OF THE Psalm above was King David, the 2nd king of Israel, who God called a man after His own heart (1 Samuel 13:14). He wrote this in repentance after falling into the sin of lust, sleeping with his friend's wife and then having the friend killed! While the Bible is open about it's heroes' failures, God does not condone their sin. One thing that made King David an amazing man of God though—is that he repented. We need to do the same.

You may not be in as deep of a sinful situation as King David was, but even the smallest amount of sin steals joy. If you are not walking in the fullness of the joy of your salvation, something has gotten in the way. Whether it's a lie you've believed, some sort of oppression from the enemy, something you need to repent of, or anything else; I am declaring now that the Holy Spirit is opening your eyes to whatever it is.

But what does salvation really mean? For David, it was being restored into right relationship with God. But that is not the only meaning. To get a good understanding, we need to look at the word used for salvation in the Bible, particularly in the New Testament, because it's usage also includes what Jesus afforded us in His death and resurrection.

Sózó Salvation

The New Testament was written in Greek and the word we understand as salvation, is sózó (Strong's number 4982 in the Greek Lexicon[1]). This word is translated into English words such as saved, delivered, healed, rescued, do well, and make whole. So God uses this word we translate as salvation for more than when our lives come into interface with Jesus.

When we need healing, God saves us. When we've fallen into a pit, even by our own digging, God saves us. When we need freedom from demons, God saves us (yes demons are real and they do afflict Christians). Salvation includes all of these things, and more. Most importantly it is the all encompassing restoration of our relationship to Father God.

As you minister:

- Salvation is God's rescue operation of coming into His creation to redeem the people around you.

- Salvation is His desire to bless people and transform every thing that is off course in their lives.

- Salvation is a work of deliverance to separate bound people from the demons they've been in bed with.

- Salvation is a healing provision, not only for a person's spirit, but for their worldly mind that is deceived and submitting to the flesh and culture more than to the Spirit of God.

- Salvation is even a healing for sickness as the Holy Spirit quickens our mortal bodies (Romans 8) and by Jesus's stripes we were healed (1 Peter 2:24).

It's not by your strength or righteousness that you minister these things, but by the grace of God, the power in Jesus's name, His blood shed for all, and the Holy Spirit who resides richly within you.

Salvation for Today

I am thankful that when this depraved and broken soul said a prayer in a religious old southern church, that salvation was not just an entry ticket to heaven. I needed freedom and healing. And I can testify that more than ever, I am getting to experience God's goodness in the land of the living (Psalm 27:13).

Salvation is for today, but more often than not, it's up to us to receive the fullness of it. This blessing, deliverance, healing, rescue, and reconciliation Jesus has already provided through His work on the cross. Unfortunately, people often only receive what they have been told they can. And so they settle for a future heaven instead of enjoying God's provision on earth.

As a side-note, we are going to talk more later about how God isn't controlling everything we experience in life. But for now, take my word that there is a part we play, a part the enemy plays, and though God knows and sees it all, He is not a puppet master pulling all our strings. The fact is, we can learn and grow in our faith and receiving all of His promises as well as ministering them to others. And when we receive what He has provided... we will have joy!

What It Really Means to be Saved

At the end of the last chapter, we prayed recognizing what God has done, what the enemy has done, what our part was, and we gave it all to Jesus. That is what some would call the sinner's prayer, or a prayer of salvation. As an evangelist on the street, I have had the joy of getting to lead people in this prayer. I want to lead many more and am still working on that!

But too often the people that I follow up with to continue in discipleship don't respond. I'm not assuming their salvation wasn't real, or that they lost it, or that what I did wasn't effective. But it's a fact that many people who profess to be Christians, and maybe even say they've given their lives to God, don't really live like their lives belong to God.

We need to help people not only give God lip service, but actually live for Him. Salvation isn't to ask Jesus to forgive our sins once, and proclaim Him as Lord during a prayer

Fullness of Joy

muttered in unison with 200 others in the room. People need to actually make Him Lord.

> *"So why do you keep calling me 'Lord, Lord!' when you don't do what I say? I will show you what it's like when someone comes to me, listens to my teaching, and then follows it. It is like a person building a house who digs deep and lays the foundation on solid rock. When the floodwaters rise and break against that house, it stands firm because it is well built."*
> Luke 6:46-48 NLT (See also John 3:36)

For many years I called Jesus Lord, but after 18 of them I ended up hating this so called Lord. I thought if He existed, He was surely evil. I had no idea what He was really like, and I had no relationship with Him. I had the shallowest of confessions of faith and the weakest prayer life, filled with doubt and anger and bed-time prayers, barely going to church, never cracking that dry Bible spine to see what His love letter actually said. But I was a "Christian." Or at least I thought I was.

Too many people are in this boat, that's why when I am talking with people, I like to ask them questions about who Jesus is to them, and why they think He came to the earth. Like I did, often they need an encounter with the living

God. I needed rescue, deliverance, healing, salvation, and so do many other "Christians." When I met Him, I got a bunch of that stuff, but what I really got was a relationship. And that is what it really means to be saved.

Salvation is laying one's life down at the feet of Jesus, giving him all the rubbish, all the filthy rags of self-righteousness, and receiving this beautiful gift that we feel absolutely unworthy of, His life. He counted the cost, and He thought you and I were worth it. He was willing to lay down His life that we might come into RELATIONSHIP with His Father, not RELIGION with something called "Christianity."

He is calling us to also lay down our lives, so others can come into this relationship with Him. Let's tell people what it really means to be saved.

Prayer

Lord Jesus, I want to walk in constant fellowship with You. I declare that You are my Lord, not only my Savior. So please instruct me, God. To the best of my ability, I will do what You say and help the people around me encounter You. When the floods and hard things in life come against me, I know You are right there to help. Right now, for the

Fullness of Joy

struggles I am facing, for the oppression of the enemy, for the healing I need in my body, soul, heart, and spirit, I pray that You would deliver me, heal me, rescue me, and really save me! Not just in the ether by a wrote prayer, but save every part of me powerfully in the here and now, and bring me into a deeper relationship with You. And thank You, Lord, that You are restoring me to the joy of my salvation. In Jesus's name I pray. Amen.

Chapter 3

The Temple and the Sacrifice

IF YOU OPEN YOUR eyes, you will notice many temples around the world. My family currently serves as missionaries in Rome. One of the ancient Romans' strategies was to subdue conquered people by assimilating their religions. The Romans didn't only erect idols and temples for the conquered people to worship Roman gods and the emperor. They also incorporated the gods of the many nations they ruled over. This is how they attempted to subdue Christianity as well. So, there are countless historical temples to thousands of gods in Rome. But even in today's sophisticated western societies, people have altars of worship, though they may not see them for what

Fullness of Joy

they are.

Curiously, we don't read of a temple in the Garden of Eden. Man and woman walked together in relationship with God, enjoying the creation He gave us stewardship over. God's plan was not to limit His goodness and interaction with His creation to a temple. He desires His people to recognize His nearness wherever they are and enjoy His blessings through relationship.

We know mankind's broken relationship with God blinded us to the spiritual realm and brought guilt, shame, and death. But Genesis 3:21 reveals God's mercy. Instead of the physical demise Adam and Eve deserved, God hid their nakedness with animal skins. You see, those sinless animals were sacrificed in place of Adam and Eve's physical death. The animal skin represented a covering for their guilt and shame.

God Steps into Our World

As God stepped into the garden in the cool of the day (Genesis 3:8), throughout history God steps into lives and interacts with us. For instance:

> *Enoch walked [in habitual fellowship] with God; and he was not, for God took him [home with Him]*
>
> Genesis 5:24 AMPC

> *Noah walked with God*
> Genesis 6:9b NKJV

This continues throughout Scripture, as well as the idea of sacrifice. As early as Genesis 4, Cain and Able gave offerings to God. And after the flood, in Genesis 8:20-21 (NLT emphasis added):

"... Noah built an altar to the Lord, and there he **sacrificed as burnt offerings** the animals and birds that had been approved for that purpose. And **the Lord was pleased with the aroma of the sacrifice** and said to himself, "I will never again curse the ground because of the human race, even though everything they think or imagine is bent toward evil from childhood. I will never again destroy all living things."

Just as Enoch walked with God, you too are called to walk with God (1 John 1:6-7). Just as Noah's sacrifice pleased God, you are called to be a living sacrifice.

> *... present your bodies as a living and holy sacrifice, acceptable to God, which is your spiritual service of worship.*
> Romans 12:1b NASB

The Moving Temple

Rather than give a complete history of the people who worshiped God, I want to briefly catch you up to Moses's

Fullness of Joy

story in Exodus. The nation of Israel at this time was a large people group without their own land. They had settled in Egypt during a famine many years before under good conditions, but over time, they became Pharaoh's slaves.

God sent a man named Moses before Pharaoh to say the famous line, "Let my people go." To which Pharaoh declines, and a series of plagues come upon Egypt because of this. Things escalate to a plague which promises to kill the first-born children, but a very special sacrifice protected God's people.

They were instructed to slay a lamb and apply it's blood to the door-post, so the angel of death would pass over instead of bringing God's wrath. The harsh slave-masters didn't have the blood covering, and their children died.

> *... without the shedding of blood, there is no forgiveness.*
> Hebrews 9:22b NLT

An amazing story follows of God parting the sea so His people could escape the chasing Egyptian army. After their rescue from captivity, God gave instructions for how to have their sins forgiven, how to make the tabernacle, and how to remember and celebrate what He had done.

Since the Israelites were wanderers, the tabernacle became a movable temple for them to worship. Something amazing happened when Moses entered this tabernacle, "...

the Lord spoke to Moses face to face, as a man speaks to his friend... (Exodus 33:11a NKJV)." (See also Exodus 26)

The Temple Destroyed...

If you're interested in more history of the temple, in 2 Samuel 7 you can read about when King David wanted to build the Lord a temple made of stone. And later God's glorious presence filling the temple Solomon built in Jerusalem, found in 2 Chronicles 7.

In the temple there was an inner area called the Holy of Holies, the Most Holy Place, where only the High Priest could enter because of God's overwhelming glory. If the priest followed instructions from God's law for his sins to be forgiven, then he could go into the Holy of Holies. Like the animal skins in Eden, Noah's burnt offerings, and the lamb slain at the first Passover in Egypt—the High Priest offered sacrifices to God so the nation's sins could be forgiven, and their deserved punishment delayed.

Stay with me, 'cause I'm heading somewhere. Let's fast forward and talk about Jesus. He made this peculiar statement to the pharisees (who were the religious leaders of His day, some of whom served in the temple Solomon built). No one understood it at first, but Jesus compared Himself to the temple and prophesied the temple would be destroyed at the same time as prophesying His death and

Fullness of Joy

resurrection (John 2:17-22).

As Jesus was hanging on the bloody cross, about to fulfill the prophecy of His death, He stated, "It is finished," and breathed His last. In that moment the sun went dark, the earth shook, dead people came out of the grave living—and a curtain *in the temple* mysteriously tore in two, from top to bottom! This veil was 60 feet wide, 30 feet high, and 4 inches thick, and was so heavy it took 300 priests to hang it. This curtain was also what separated people from the Most Holy Place of God's presence. But when Christ died, the barrier to the Holy of Holies rent open.

> *... we can boldly enter heaven's Most Holy Place because of the blood of Jesus. By his death, Jesus opened a new and life-giving way through the curtain into the Most Holy Place. And since we have a great High Priest who rules over God's house, let us go right into the presence of God with sincere hearts fully trusting him. For our guilty consciences have been sprinkled with Christ's blood to make us clean, and our bodies have been washed with pure water.*
> Hebrews 10:19-22 NLT

Jesus was called the lamb of God who takes away the sins of the world (John 1:29, 1 Peter 1:19-20, 1 Corinthians 5:7,

Revelation 5 and 13:8). Hebrews 8-10 shows that Jesus is now our High Priest, and He has made a way for us to enter into the Holy of Holies—not by the blood of a common lamb, but by His own precious blood, that of the sinless Son of God.

... the Temple resurrected!

Not many years after Jesus's resurrection, in A.D. 70, the physical temple in Jerusalem was destroyed. But the amazing truth is that it has been resurrected in everyone who gives their life to Jesus. When you allowed Jesus to come into your heart and save you, the presence of God filled you, and you became His temple. This is how close God is with you.

> *Do you not know that you are the temple of God and that the Spirit of God dwells in you?*
> 1 Corinthians 3:16 NKJV
> (See also chapter 6:15-20)

The bottom line is God always desires to meet with us. Jesus was called Immanuel, which means God with us (Matthew 1:23). And even towards the end the Bible, we read that God is going to make His dwelling place with man (Revelation 21:3).

You, believer, carry the presence of God, and this should give you great joy!

Fullness of Joy

You will make known to me the way of life; In Your presence is fullness of joy; In Your right hand there are pleasures forever.

Psalm 16:11 NASB

Prayer

God, it's clear throughout Biblical history that You've fought for a relationship with mankind over and over. Despite our sin, You always made a way to walk with us. Through Jesus, I have also entered into relationship with You. Thank You, precious Lamb of God who takes away the sins of the world. Thank you for dwelling in me, Holy Spirit, and that I carry your glory like the tabernacle. Please help my life to exemplify a habitation of your presence. Not just the innermost part of my spirit, but all throughout this temple. I want to be utterly purified and set apart for You. I want to live my life in recognition that You are always with me—leading me, cleansing me, desiring relationship, that we would talk face to face, and that we would walk with one another. What an honor this is. Thank You, Lord!

Chapter 4

Living as a Child of God and Joint-Heir with Christ

And you He made alive, who were dead in trespasses and sins, in which you once walked according to the course of this world, according to the prince of the power of the air, the spirit who now works in the sons of disobedience, among whom also we all once conducted ourselves in the lusts of our flesh, fulfilling the desires of the flesh and of the mind, and were by nature children of wrath,

Fullness of Joy

> *just as the others.*
> *But God, who is rich in mercy, because of His great love with which He loved us, even when we were dead in trespasses, made us alive together with Christ (by grace you have been saved), and raised us up together, and made us sit together in the heavenly places in Christ Jesus, that in the ages to come He might show the exceeding riches of His grace in His kindness toward us in Christ Jesus. For by grace you have been saved through faith, and that not of yourselves; it is the gift of God, not of works, lest anyone should boast. For we are His workmanship, created in Christ Jesus for good works, which God prepared beforehand that we should walk in them.*
>
> Ephesians 2:1-10 NKJV

THE ABOVE PASSAGE SHOWS that before we gave our lives to Jesus, we were dead in our sin, led by our lusts and worldly desires, and children of disobedience and wrath. I can attest that this is an accurate description of my life before Christ. But even those who don't remember a Sunday morning or Wednesday night outside of church, who think they don't have a flashy testimony, were still at one time "sons of disobedience" (see also Colossians 3:6-11 NKJV).

Being raised with Christian moral values, learning about God and believing in Him, hearing sermons, reading the Bible, and having some sort of prayer life, are invaluable. But if we haven't truly been born of the Spirit, we continue to be children of wrath. Think of the Pharisees, they did all these religious things, but Jesus called them sons of the devil (John 8:41-47). Why? Because they did not recognize what God was doing right in front of their eyes. Jesus was God manifested in the flesh, and the Pharisees wanted to kill him. They had a form of godliness, but it did not emanate from the One they supposedly worshiped.

This reveals that even though the Pharisees had all the religious systems appearing perfect to keep them in good standing with God, the vast majority of them had no relationship with the living God. And I hate to break it to you, but this is where many Christians stand as well. We need to recognize if we are playing religion, or if we have been brought into the family.

But God Adopted Us

So then, beloved ones, the flesh has no claims on us at all, and we have no further obligation to live in obedience to it. For when you live

Fullness of Joy

> *controlled by the flesh, you are about to die. But if the life of the Spirit puts to death the corrupt ways of the flesh, we then taste His abundant life. The mature children of God are those who are moved by the impulses of the Holy Spirit. And you did not receive the "spirit of religious duty," leading you back into the fear of never being good enough. But you have received the "Spirit of full acceptance," enfolding you into the family of God. And you will never feel orphaned, for as He rises up within us, our spirits join Him in saying the words of tender affection, "Beloved Father!"*
> Romans 8:12-15 TPT

Adopted by God. This is your standing when you have accepted Christ as your Lord and Savior, and truly been born again. He has placed His life-giving Spirit in you, and this is meant to bring you back into the nature humanity was never meant to leave. It is to be like God—as His child.

Anyone who has adopted a child knows it's not an easy process. It is long, hard, costly, and full of ups and downs. Though worth it, the parents are often required a hefty financial investment, and a laying down of part of their lives. Unfortunately, many adopted children continue to carry with them all sorts of baggage from the life they had before. Often they don't feel the love and investment that their new parents have poured out. They still feel the wounds of their old life. And they act on this.

We do this in our Christian walk in similar ways. Even as we are told the good news of our adoption, the enemy whispers that we are still orphans. We've been brought into a kingdom, and exchanged filthy rags for robes of righteousness. But if we never learn how to act in this kingdom, we will continue to act like thieves and beggars. We have been given a signet ring that says we are a child of the King. There's incomprehensible power behind that ring. But we continue to act like sons of the devil and children of wrath.

Joint-Heirs with Christ

This signet ring your Heavenly Father places on your finger is the same ring Jesus has. Yet many pastors continue to drone doctrines of unworthiness and depravity, as if you are a second-class child, or more like a worm. The enemy is happy to side with this false religion to convince you that transformation can only happen when you die.

That old father of lies—Satan—will do anything to keep us from feeling our true Heavenly Father's love. And so we are somehow sure God grudgingly did what was needed to save us. Not because He thought we were worthy of His Son's life, but because He didn't have a choice, and now

Fullness of Joy

He's stuck with us.

If we believe these lies, we become the "child" that acts like the unloved servant or slave of the household, even as God made us joint-heirs with Jesus. Even despite the fact that He proved His great love by giving Christ to die for our redemption (John 3:16, Romans 8:17-19, 28-32).

Do you know what this means? Everything the first-born Son, Jesus, has as an inheritance, is also given to you. Though you did nothing to deserve it, the Father raised you up and seated you with Christ in Heavenly places, at His righteous right hand. You probably would feel awkward sitting on a throne next to Almighty God, Creator of everything, the Beginning and the End. But He places you there, and says, "Rule with me."

> *To Him who loved us and washed us from our sins in His own blood, and has made us kings and priests to His God and Father, to Him be glory and dominion forever and ever. Amen.*
> Revelation 1:5b-6 NKJV (see also Rev. 4:21 and Eph. 2:6 again from the start of this chapter)

Child of God

Knowing this and the fact that God originally created humanity in His image (Genesis 1:27-28 and Psalm 8:3-6), it's inexcusable to live like anything but a child of God. And when we really grasp this, we will have such joy. In the light of our good God calling us His own, the shadow of what we once were—and all the depravity, fear, and sorrow—has to go.

Look at the Son of God and the way He acted. You will see a man who was unafraid of the world, the religious "leaders," and the system. He is closer than a brother, has compassion on the weakest, points out the faith of the worldly, and recognizes the generosity of the poorest. He walked on water, through walls, and escaped amid angry mobs. He was a wild man of faith in the desert, a preacher to thousands, and a miracle worker. And one day He will ride down through the clouds on a white horse, with flames in His eyes, bearing the name Faithful and True.

Jesus is beautiful. And you are called to be like Him.

Prayer

Father God, thank You for adopting me away from the father of lies. I am no longer a child of disobedience and headed towards wrath. You have called me Your very own, placed Your Spirit within me, and gave me the same inheritance of Your only begotten Son. Please heal my heart and my mind of all the old baggage of my previous life. I want to be like Jesus. I want to hold His desires, His thoughts, His feelings, His ways. Please empower me and teach me how to live as a child of God and joint-heir with Christ.

Chapter 5

You Are More Like Christ than Fallen Adam

The Scriptures tell us, "The first man, Adam, became a living person." But the last Adam— that is, Christ—is a life-giving Spirit. What comes first is the natural body, then the spiritual body comes later. Adam, the first man, was made from the dust of the earth, while Christ, the second man, came from heaven. Earthly people are like the earthly man, and heavenly people are like the

> *heavenly man. Just as we are now like the earthly man, we will someday be like the heavenly man.*
>
> 1 Corinthians 15:14-49 NLT

OFTEN WE DON'T HAVE joy because we still think of ourselves as fallen and we aren't receiving what God has made available. We should no longer think of ourselves as like Adam, because we have been born again into the likeness of the last Adam who was Christ.

A big problem in the church is we're often taught to apply the Bible from the perspective of people who are unredeemed, believers who are not Spirit-filled, and even people who are demonized! Maybe you are doing better than this, but as you read about the disciples and Jesus in Scripture, who do you really identify with more?

It's true we are like all these Biblical figures at different times in our lives, and I have been literally changed for the better through their stories. But my point is, as we're reading about Jesus in the gospels, we should think, "I want to be like Him." Not only should we desire that, but I am convinced that His intention is that we actually become like Him.

John W. Nichols

The Broken, the Friend, the Prideful, and the Minister

Mark 2:1-12 tells the story of Jesus preaching in a home where people crowded around Him so much there was no room to even come near the door of the house. Outside was a paralytic and some men who decided if they could just get to Jesus, then the man who could not walk would be healed. They were so determined, they brought the man and his bed on the roof, broke through a section, and lowered him before Jesus! Can you imagine listening to Jesus preaching the Word, and suddenly the roof is coming apart, and a man on a bed is dropped down?

Meanwhile, by the Holy Spirit, Jesus is always aware of the hearts of the people. He sees some are in faith, and some aren't. There are some people in the crowd who are skeptics, and they don't trust that Jesus is from God. But Jesus looks at this paralytic and his four friends, and says because of their faith, his sins are forgiven.

Jesus was not only ministering to the man, but He's picking a fight with the attending scribes who were prideful and unable to accept the new thing God was doing. Because they couldn't see Jesus was the Son of God, they thought He was blaspheming by forgiving the man's sins. Knowing their hearts, Jesus says,

> "*Which is easier, to say to the paralytic, 'Your*

> *sins are forgiven you,' or to say, 'Arise, take up your bed and walk'? But that you may know that the Son of Man has power on earth to forgive sins"—He said to the paralytic, "I say to you, arise, take up your bed, and go to your house." Immediately he arose, took up the bed, and went out in the presence of them all, so that all were amazed and glorified God, saying, "We never saw anything like this!"*
> Mark 2:9-12 NKJV

Back in that day, it definitely was not easier to say your sins are forgiven. But today in a lot of the modern Christian churches, people would say, "It's easier to say your sins are forgiven. Forgiveness of sins is easy. I get that by default. And theology has taught us the verses about healing are really just about sins being forgiven anyway." Not to mention, you can't see sins being forgiven, so we can just assume it's happening, and not have to prove anything in the natural like a life being transformed—let alone the healing of paralysis.

There is a grace movement in much of the church with parts that are good, but also a hyper-grace that excuses Christians to be just like the world, and indulge in almost any type of sin, assuming they are forgiven. But God intends us to live in a manner worthy of the gospel (Philippians 1:21-30). His grace is meant to lead us out of sin and empower us into the life of Christ.

When we listen to the story above, we often relate to a few different people. Maybe we relate to the man who is in desperate need of Jesus's healing. Maybe we relate to the friends who are bringing that man before Jesus. We might think, "Yeah, we're helping people get to Jesus, so that they can be healed." Since you're reading this book, you probably don't relate to the prideful scribes who are looking for a chance to prove Jesus was a heretic. But some will relate to those people, if they're honest.

You know what I'm getting at. You are meant to relate to Jesus. And Jesus was the one ministering. The one who caused people to gasp, "Oh, you can't say that." You can't stand in the place of Jehovah Hashopet (The Lord, The Judge) and forgive sins. How dare you? That's too far. Do you think you're God?

But Jesus said to His disciples, "Peace be to you; just as the Father has sent Me, I also send you." And when He had said this, He breathed on them and said to them, "Receive the Holy Spirit. If you forgive the sins of any, their sins have been forgiven them; if you retain the sins of any, they have been retained (John 20:21-23 NASB)."

Like the One Who Sent You

You are called to be like Christ. This is what Jesus

Fullness of Joy

taught His disciples to do and prophesied would happen.

> *"I tell you the truth, anyone who believes in me will do the same works I have done, and even greater works, because I am going to be with the Father. You can ask for anything in my name, and I will do it, so that the Son can bring glory to the Father. Yes, ask me for anything in my name, and I will do it!"*
> John 14:12-14 NLT

> *And then He told them, "Go into all the world and preach the Good News to everyone. Anyone who believes and is baptized will be saved. But anyone who refuses to believe will be condemned. These miraculous signs will accompany those who believe: They will cast out demons in my name, and they will speak in new languages. They will be able to handle snakes with safety, and if they drink anything poisonous, it won't hurt them. They will be able to place their hands on the sick, and they will be healed." When the Lord Jesus had finished talking with them, He was taken up into heaven and sat down in the place of honor at God's right hand. And the disciples went everywhere and preached, and the Lord*

worked through them, confirming what they said by many miraculous signs.
Mark 16:15-20 NLT

Notice the end of the gospel of Mark opens up Jesus's impartation to all believers, not just His original apostles. That means us. We are to minister in the same ways Jesus did. As we preach the gospel, we should expect there to be signs following. We should expect miracles.

This is what Jesus (and His disciples after Him) did:

- He went about preaching the kingdom of God, and revealing the Father.
- He delivered people from demons and destroyed the works of the devil (1 John 3:8).
- He healed the sick, and did wonderful acts.
- He laid down His life, and glorified the One who sent Him.

Discerning Good and Evil

You are not meant to be under the bondage of the devil and acting just like everyone else in this fallen world. You are not meant to be afraid of the devil, not willing to face the retaliation that comes with spiritual warfare and deliverance. You are not meant to be oblivious to the works of the devil and make room for them. Just as "God anointed

Fullness of Joy

Jesus of Nazareth with the Holy Spirit and with power, who went about doing good and healing all who were oppressed by the devil, for God was with Him (Acts 10:38)," so are you.

When we look at John 5:16-47, we see Jesus heal another paralytic and this time the religious leaders were mad because He "worked on the Sabbath." Jesus's response to their anger was amazing. He said His Father is always at work, and He had to do what He saw His Father doing.

This is another example of how we need to be. First of all, when we look at the world around us, we need to discern what the enemy is doing and what God is doing. Next, we need to care more about what God Our Father is doing, and less about what the religious system says is normal. Even to step out in faith and see God move beyond our capabilities. If this is so far outside your comfort zone and your realm of belief, you need to expand your thinking.

Jesus wants you to carry on what He purchased for you. He wants you to perceive what the Father is doing. He wants you to experience the relationship He had with the Father. He wants to impart to you the same anointing that He walked in.

I declare that as you read these words you are receiving a boldness to ignore everyone else's thoughts in favor of your Heavenly Father's. You are receiving boldness to anger the dead religious leaders, pick a fight with the devil, and even to disappoint friends, so that you can give your life as a sacrifice. Just as Jesus was willing to call out Satan speaking through His friend Peter, when he tried to sway Him from God's plans (Matt. 16:21-28), so you will be willing to call out the enemy's voice speaking through your friends and family.

Jesus never feared any man. He had complete confidence in who He was as the Son of God. Child of God, you too need to have complete confidence in who you are. The Father has proven His love, and sent you. So have faith to do what Jesus did, and to act like Jesus acted.

Prayer

> *Father God, I'm sorry for the ways that I've lived like fallen Adam, or like the demonized, or the Pharisees, or even your disciples, who were constantly putting their feet in their mouths. God, please forgive me for looking at all these people and identifying with them in their brokenness; overlooking all the wonderful verses and passages in the Bible that clearly show me who you desire me to be. I want to copy You. I don't want to copy the world. I don't want to copy anyone else in the Bible. Yes, I thank You that I can learn from*

Fullness of Joy

them, but ultimately I want to be transformed to be like You. Thank You God, that as I live the life You created me to live, looking into Your perfect face, I will one day find that I look like You. I thank You that right now I am being transformed from glory to glory into Your image and likeness.

Chapter 6

Experiencing the Fullness of Joy

Good Father

IN ORDER TO HAVE joy rooted deep down in our souls, and overflowing out of our hearts, we need a deeper and deeper revelation of our Heavenly Father's goodness. In Mark 10:18 (NASB) Jesus said, "Why do you call Me good? No one is good except God alone."

If Jesus (who never sinned) says this, how good is the Father? Immeasurably good. His goodness is beyond your imagination. If you are confused about His goodness, I encourage you to start regularly spending time with the Lord. Wait on Him, listen to Him, and He will show you His goodness. He will show you His love. He'll speak things to you that will blow your mind.

If you've gone through a lot of hard things in your life, I encourage you to get my free book, *God is Here: Finding God in the Pain of a Broken World*. This will help you allow God to heal your heart, really know His goodness, and be assured He is with you and loves you.

One time when Jesus was talking about the goodness of His Father, He said,

> "Ask, and it will be given to you; seek, and you will find; knock, and it will be opened to you. For everyone who asks receives, and the one who seeks finds, and to the one who knocks it will be opened. Or what person is there among you who, when his son asks for a loaf of bread, will give him a stone? Or if he asks for a fish, he will not give him a snake, will he? So if you, despite being evil, know how to give good gifts to your children, how much more will your Father who is in heaven give good things to those who ask Him!"
> Matthew 7:7-11 NASB

You know, the Father cares very much about your heart. He loves you and cares about what you care about. He sees your desires, and He wants to give you the best version of those things. Just like most earthly fathers try to do good by their children, your Heavenly Father who has not one bit of evil in Him, wants to do good by you. As you soak in this confidence of God's goodness, joy will flow out of your heart into your thoughts, words, and actions.

Joy Is an Essential Element of Faith

One time in a prayer meeting I was helping facilitate, the Holy Spirit began to move on a portion of the people in the room, and they experienced a deep joy and laughter in the Lord. As I was encouraging the others to join, I realized some of them were frowning. As they were crying out to the Lord, they looked like they didn't believe He was going to answer their prayers. I had to remind them, "Smile! Turn your frown upside down!"

If you're praying and you sound hopeless, something is off. If you feel as if you need to beg God to do something good, you still need a deeper revelation of His goodness. Joy comes through faith. Faith—really believing to the deepest core of your being in who God is and who He says you are—will give you joy.

If everything that we've talked about has not put a smile on your face. I don't know what will. Seriously, get happy. Turn your frown upside down. Smile. You will be amazed at what it does if you just make your face smile. You can

Fullness of Joy

have joy.

I'm not talking about faking it. And I'm not talking about surface happiness. True joy is deeper than our circumstances. If only because of the goodness of our God, we can smile, even in the face of our trials. We can command our soul to bless the Lord and to have joy.

Proverbs 17:22 says, "A joyful heart is a good medicine, but a broken spirit dries up the bones (NASB)."

I don't know about you but I want good medicine. I don't want my bones to be dried up, so I'm gonna have a joyful heart. But sometimes I have to realize that my heart is not being joyful. And that's when I tell it what to do.

Often we allow our circumstances, our senses, and the chemicals in our brains to tell us what we feel. Those are faulty tools to measure reality, and we shouldn't be led by them. Who we are and the Biblical truth we live by is greater than these imperfect guides. And our God is far and away greater. His promises are more powerful. All those things must bow at the sound of His name. So we need to command our emotions, our way of thinking, our body, and even our circumstances to get in line with the truth of God's Word.

Jesus Is Absolutely Joyful

We can always have joy because Jesus is with us and in

His presence is fullness of joy (as we've quoted before from Psalm 16). Really recognize this—Jesus is joyful! I have had so many times of personal prayer where the Holy Spirit floods my heart with incomprehensible joy. There have been many times where I and my friends were praying in my living room, and we experienced something that can only be described as holy laughter. It was like Jesus came in the room and said, "Let's party."

Yes, Jesus feels deeply grieved at times. And He can be very serious and stern. There can be fire in His eyes, and a sword from His mouth. I've heard His voice like the sound of many waters no one would dare cross. But I've also seen the most beautiful smile you will ever see. I've heard the most contagious laugh you will ever hear. And anyone who knows Him will tell you He has the best sense of humor.

Did you ever recognize the first miracle Jesus did was turning water into wine? This is not a wine commercial by the way, I don't drink alcohol. I used to, but I stopped when I decided to receive my joy and comfort by the Holy Spirit. The Bible says not to get drunk on wine, but to be filled with the Holy Spirit (Ephesians 5:18). But as He did in His first miracle, Jesus has new wine.

Fullness of Joy

"What you see was predicted long ago by the prophet Joel..."

Shortly after Jesus's ascension, His followers were waiting in prayer for the promise of the Holy Spirit to descend. Guess what happened after the ruckus of God's mighty wind and holy fire coming upon His devotees? Everyone assumed they were drunk. It wasn't because they were drinking the wine of this world. It was because they were drinking Jesus's new wine. This is confirmed when Peter states Joel 2 predicted what would happen when the Holy Spirit would be poured out (Acts 2:1-21).

Just a few verses before the part of Joel which Peter quoted, God spoke through the prophet these words, "*Be glad* then, you children of Zion, *And rejoice in the Lord your God*; For He has given you the former rain faithfully, And He will cause the rain to come down for you— The former rain, And the latter rain in the first month. The threshing floors shall be full of wheat, And *the vats shall overflow with new wine* and oil (Joel 2:23-24 NKJV emphasis added)."

Believe it or not, experiences of great joy and laughter, like Jesus's followers had in the upper room, are recorded by various people throughout history, especially during revivals which brought deep transformation in the people who were touched by God. There was a time in my life when

I wasn't sure about these outbreaks in church services and prayer meetings. I didn't know if they were genuinely a move of the Holy Spirit.

But I'm thankful to have now experienced it first-hand, and I've since been in many prayer meetings where we were overcome with extreme joy. It wasn't contrived or manufactured, but it was hard to contain, and wonderfully contagious. Seriously, my stomach and mouth felt sore afterwards from the prolonged hearty laughter. And where I used to think God would never bring "disorder" to a church service, I have to recognize God's idea of order based on Acts 2 looks quite different than most religious people's idea of what should or should not take place in a gathering of the saints.

More than give you theology or try to wrap your head around it, I can simply tell you, Jesus throws the best parties. I've laughed harder in times with Jesus than I ever did when I was doing drugs and alcohol. I've tasted and seen His new wine, and it's so much better than anything in this world. His Spirit is so much better than the spirits that are in alcoholic beverages. If you haven't, you should taste and see for yourself.

What if Jesus came to your prayer session and wanted to party? Remember, He's happy. He has a good idea of how this all will turn out. And I too have read ahead to the end of the Book (the Bible), and can let you in on a little secret.

Fullness of Joy

We win! If Jesus wants to celebrate His victory, and pours out His new wine, don't withhold your cup.

He's not too concerned about being dignified and doesn't care what the onlookers think. He wants your cup to overflow and He doesn't mind making a mess. I dare you to drink in His Spirit. To let Him fill your cup with new wine, and experience His overwhelming joy.

Prayer

Father God, thank You that even as the enemy plans evil, You sit in the heavens and laugh (Psalms 2:4). Holy Spirit, thank You that bearing Your fruit includes joy (Galatians 5:22). Jesus, I want to look in Your eyes and see joy. I want to be captivated by the most contagious smile the world has ever seen. I want my cup to overflow with Your new wine. After this prayer, I am going to close my eyes and picture You smiling as You pour out Your joy. I believe my cup will overflow and I will never be the same, in Your name I pray, amen!

Chapter 7

Being a Person of Faith, Hope, and Love

For now we see but a faint reflection of riddles and mysteries as though reflected in a mirror, but one day we will see face-to-face. My understanding is incomplete now, but one day I will understand everything, just as everything about me has been fully understood. Until then, there are three things that remain: faith, hope, and love—yet love surpasses them all. So above all else, let love be the beautiful prize for which you run.

1 Corinthians 13:12-13 TPT

Fullness of Joy

WE'VE SPENT SOME TIME talking about what God has done for you and who you are in Christ. A profound revelation of this will lead you into a life marked by faith, hope, and love. One of these subjects could be a chapter—or even a book—in itself, but for the sake of brevity we will dip into each of them here.

Faith

> *So faith comes from hearing, that is, hearing the Good News about Christ.*
> Romans 10:17 NLT

> *And without faith it is impossible to please Him, for the one who comes to God must believe that He exists, and that He proves to be One who rewards those who seek Him.*
> Hebrews 11:6 NASB

A person comes into faith when hearing the Word of God, and actively trusting that Word with their whole being. Like His Father who sent Him, Jesus was able to keenly discern true faith in people's hearts. God knows if we have faith when we come to Him. We might be able to fool others, or even ourselves, but we can't fool Him. And we can't please Him without faith. First of all, believing in Him, and secondly believing He rewards us who seek Him.

John W. Nichols

> *So Jesus answered and said to them, "Have faith in God. For assuredly, I say to you, whoever says to this mountain, 'Be removed and be cast into the sea,' and does not doubt in his heart, but believes that those things he says will be done, he will have whatever he says. Therefore I say to you, whatever things you ask when you pray, believe that you receive them, and you will have them.*
> Mark 11:22-24 NKJV

Because of your faith in Jesus, you have become a child of God, and the Bible says that the Holy Spirit, the same power that raised Christ from the dead, inhabits you (Romans 8:9-11, Eph. 1:17-21). Recognize this, the same One who created everything with the power of His voice fills you! So yes, when you speak in faith over mountains, and you speak over circumstances, they will change. Your faith can transform your life.

What hinders us is doubt. We must rid our hearts of every lingering unbelief. We need to really believe that the promises God has given us are true. They're more true than our circumstances. They're more true than what we can see in the natural realm around us.

> *Now faith is the assurance (the confirmation, the title deed) of the things [we] hope for,*

Fullness of Joy

> *being the proof of things [we] do not see and the conviction of their reality [faith perceiving as real fact what is not revealed to the senses].*
> Hebrews 11:1 AMPC

Not only does this verse validate the reality of the unseen, it says *now* faith is. Faith is active now. Often, when we ask God to do something, we think our answer might come, rather than confidently believing He has already answered and He is at work. Even when we don't see God's answer in the natural, we need to believe that we have it.

Trust me, it's not always faith when we say, "I believe." And definitely not when we say, "I'll believe it when I see it." True belief and faith is living according to something, even taking action, no matter what we see. We praise God before the manifestation of our request. We know He will answer because our God is good, and He takes good care of us. That's the kind of faith Jesus recognized so many times in the gospels and attributed it to various people receiving miracles. And it's the kind of faith we need to have.

Hope

Even when we're going through the hardest trials hope says that we're going to come out of it, that God is turning these hardships around for our good. Because we love God and we're called according to His purposes, we can always hope for good things (Romans 8:28).

Some people always have a negative outlook. They constantly think about bad things that could happen and assume they will. Because it has become a habitual way of thinking, they continue to do this no matter how often they are proven wrong! Maybe you know someone like this (hopefully not someone you see every day in the mirror).

Hasn't God proven over and over that He is taking good care of you? If you continually think something bad is going to happen to you, or that things aren't going to work out, I want you to have a dose of hope. As you're reading this I pray you will have a hope transfusion. You will start to look into the future, you will see good things, and you will declare those good things!

Whenever you start to feel hopeless, or negative prophecy creeps into your thoughts and words, turn it on its head. Instead of proclaiming something bad is going to happen, proclaim the opposite. Declare that good things are coming your way.

> *She is clothed with strength and dignity, and she laughs without fear of the future.*
> Proverbs 31:25 NLT

I like to think of hope as expectation of good things to come. It's important that you picture these things. Part of you, that was created in the image of God, is your imagination. It's powerful! If you are always picturing things going wrong, it's very likely that you will reap those bad things. But if you are imagining the good that God has in store for you, your faith will increase. This helps you to receive from Him.

Love

> *If I have the gift of prophecy, and know all mysteries and all knowledge; and if I have all faith, so as to remove mountains, but do not have love, I am nothing.*
> 1 Corinthians 13:2 NASB

Love is the most important thing. Without it, our faith and hope would be built on a foundation of selfishness. Our hope would be solely set on our own future, and our faith would lay hold of our own pleasure. We would be willing to trample over anyone to attain our desires.

> *You are to love the Lord Yahweh, your God, with a passionate heart, from the depths of your soul, with your every thought, and with all your strength. This is the great and supreme commandment. And the second is this: 'You must love your neighbor in the same way you love yourself.' You will never find a*

greater commandment than these.
Mark 12:30-31 TPT

True love is loving God and people. It causes us to submit to Him, and to see the people around us through His eyes. It protects us from selfishly hoping only in our own future, and guards our faith from only seeking our own joy. Love will cause us to be about the true joy of the people around us. And most importantly it will lead us to desire to please the Father's heart.

As Jesus was instructing His disciples for when He wasn't going to be with them anymore, He said, "A new commandment I give to you, that you love one another; as I have loved you, that you also love one another. By this all will know that you are My disciples, if you have love for one another (John 13:34-35 NKJV)."

When someone encounters a born-again Christian, they should be first of all struck by their love. And as that loving person shares the God-stories in their life, when they are expressing the world's need to come to Jesus, and pleading for whoever they are talking with to give their life to Him—all must flow from a place of love.

Even as we confront sinful habits, it must communicate, *God wants better for you. God cares so much about you. He has better for you than a life of brokenness and sin.* This is not out of condemnation, or saying, "You are a bad person," or "Your behavior is annoying me," or "I wish you would go away or be like someone else." But saying, "I love you because God loves you with an everlasting love—a love that will go to uncomfortable places to free you to live the life God created you for."

Prayer

> *Lord, thank You that You are making a way for me to be a person of Your love, Your faith, and Your hope. Please forgive me for ever doubting or giving in to hopelessness, Jesus. I recognize it is ultimately showing the weakness of my faith and trust in You and Your goodness. And I pray that when You come to me, You wouldn't say You have not been able to find faith (Luke 18:1-8). I ask You to dispel everything that is inhibiting me, right now, and bind to my heart supernatural faith, hope, and love! I pray You would find in me a person of faith and love, who has not only partaken in, but also shared Your hope in love. Amen!*

Chapter 8

Understanding Water Baptism

What shall we say then? Shall we continue in sin that grace may abound? Certainly not! How shall we who died to sin live any longer in it? Or do you not know that as many of us as were baptized into Christ Jesus were baptized into His death? Therefore we were buried with Him through baptism into death, that just as Christ was raised from the dead by the glory of the Father, even so we also should walk in newness of life.

Romans 6:1-4 NKJV (read also verses 5-11)

Fullness of Joy

A LOT OF PEOPLE don't really understand water baptism. I heard a funny story from a friend who was a Muslim before coming to Christ. When he was invited to church, they took communion but didn't offer him any, and he thought they were being racist. But then he was even more surprised when he saw people getting into a bath with their clothes on, in front of everyone!

We'll talk more about communion in an upcoming book in this series, but what my friend didn't know about baptism is that it is a public proclamation of our faith in Christ. It is declaring our allegiance and submission to our Lord and Savior, Jesus the Son of God, who died and rose again. And there is something deeper happening than merely getting plunged into water. This is a prophetic act which should be transformative, and not only natural, but supernatural.

Like the Scriptures above reveal, baptism is meant to show that we are dying to ourselves and our old way of life, and being born again into Christ's life and ways. As we are submerged into the waters of baptism it is both a representation and a spiritual reality of being carried with Jesus into His death and burial. Then as we come out of the waters, this is not only a picture, but an all-encompassing truth, that we have been raised in Christ's resurrection.

Therefore, baptism is vital, even though Scripture reveals it isn't a requirement to go to heaven. In Luke

23:32-43, we read the amazing story of a man hanging next to Jesus on his own cross. This criminal recognized who Jesus really was. Despite that this man had no opportunity to be baptized before he died, the Savior of the World said He would see him that day in paradise.

Although baptism isn't a pre-requisite for salvation, it is nonetheless important. If nothing else it is a powerful reference when you are fighting to overcome sin and the accusations of the enemy. Remembering the day you were baptized, you can boldly proclaim, "No, that is not who I am anymore. That old me has died, and it is no longer I who live, but Christ lives in me." (See Galatians 2:17-21)

New Testament Examples

We can look at some different stories about baptism in the Gospels and Acts. Probably the most important is recorded before Jesus started what we think of as His earthly ministry (Matthew 3:11-17, Mark 1:9-11, Luke 3:21-23, John 1:19-34). The prophet, John the Baptist, was baptizing people in the Jordan River, and he received a revelation of Jesus being the Lamb of God who would baptize in the Holy Spirit and fire. So, when Jesus said it was necessary for Him to be baptized, John didn't feel worthy to do it. But Jesus was showing us how we are supposed to live. As John baptized Him, the Holy Spirit

Fullness of Joy

descended upon Jesus and the voice of God declared He is His beloved Son.

Jesus is our example, and we read after His baptism in Luke 4:1 (NASB), "Now Jesus, full of the Holy Spirit, returned from the Jordan and was led around by the Spirit in the wilderness..." Some other translations render this as "filled with the Holy Spirit." We should expect a similar filling of the Holy Spirit and His leading as we are baptized.

Jesus then displayed further obedience and walking as a living sacrifice, as He fasted in the desert 40 days and 40 nights, and overcame the temptations of the devil with the Word of God. Afterwards we read in Luke 4:14a (NASB), "And Jesus returned to Galilee in the power of the Spirit..." This *power* is distinguished from how He entered the desert, and we should expect the power of the Holy Spirit to come upon us as well when we are submitted to God and willing to die to ourselves.

Jesus still baptizes, not in water, but in the Holy Spirit and in fire, and these are other baptisms which we should seek to receive from Him. We'll talk about these things in later books in this series. For now, if you want to know about and receive the baptism in the Holy Spirit, you can download and read my free PDF that comes with the workbook called, *Navigating the Maze of Life with God* (also linked in the Introduction).

Although water baptism is separate from these baptisms

performed by Jesus, it is still important as we see the disciples continue to perform water baptisms in Acts after Jesus's ascension. The earliest record is on the day of Pentecost when Peter is preaching:

> *"Each of you must repent of your sins and turn to God, and be baptized in the name of Jesus Christ for the forgiveness of your sins. Then you will receive the gift of the Holy Spirit. This promise is to you, to your children, and to those far away—all who have been called by the Lord our God."*
> Acts 2:38-39 NLT

We learn in this passage that baptism is a sign of repentance and leads to forgiveness of sins. It also corroborates that the gift of the Holy Spirit is available to us when we are baptized. We continue to read many examples of people receiving the gospel, including Samaritans and Gentiles, and then being baptized and receiving the Holy Spirit in Acts 8:5-40; 9:10-19; 10:47-48; 16:13-34; 18:5-8; 19:1-6; 22:14-17.

Baptism Is for Today

In all these examples we do not read of any people taking a course before being baptized. They didn't follow the apostles for a year and learn all the deep mysteries of baptism. They didn't prove the steadfastness of their hearts to the Lord. They responded quickly.

In one of these accounts (Acts 8:25-40 NKJV), an Ethiopian eunuch who just barely began to understand the gospel, sees water and asks, "What hinders me from being baptized?" A similar thing happened to me when I began to understand the gospel, I had an inexplicable and urgent desire to be water-baptized.

It was after my baptism that everything turned around, and although not perfectly by any means, I started living a different life. Because of the doctrine of that particular church, I didn't learn of deliverance from the many demons I still struggled with, or the fact that we can live a holy life, or about the gift of the Holy Spirit. But I never lost my pursuit and devotion to the Lord. My life was radically marked and changed from that moment forward.

In Acts 19:1-6 we read of Paul baptizing some men who had been previously baptized by John the Baptist. I have since been baptized again after what was mentioned in the previous paragraph. Just as these men didn't have the full revelation, I believe it matters who baptizes you and what is being imparted at the time of baptism.

I had been baptized as an infant in the Catholic church and the Presbyterian church. While I appreciate my parents attempt to dedicate me to the Lord, my life did not bear the fruit of baptism. At 20 years of age, I was baptized in the church mentioned before and it was beautiful in many ways. I believe this baptism was more powerful because it was my own choice—a response to the nudging of the Holy Spirit and my personal faith in Jesus.

But even after being saved for 20 years and going into full-time ministry, I wanted to be baptized again. It wasn't because I felt like the other one didn't take. It was because I knew the church where I was baptized had many wrong doctrines and they could only offer me a part of the gospel. This pastor taught that manifestations of the Holy Spirit today are demonically inspired.

Although these men in Acts 19 had a piece of revelation from John the Baptist, the repentance of sins, "On hearing this they were baptized [again, this time] in the name of the Lord Jesus. And as Paul laid his hands upon them, the Holy Spirit came on them; and they spoke in [foreign, unknown] tongues (languages) and prophesied (Acts 19:5-6 AMPC)." It would have been impossible for that pastor to offer me what Paul offered these men, when the church's basic doctrine was unbiblical.

My encouragement to you is to be baptized as soon as possible if you have not been already. And if you have been, what were you baptized into before? The Lord knows and is gracious, and He will use anything that you've given Him to help you come into His plans for your life. But if it be

Fullness of Joy

possible, even if it means humbling yourself, receive all you can from Him today.

Prayer

> *Thank You, Jesus, for the perfect life You lived, and for Your death on the cross where You bore my sins. Thank You for carrying my sins into the grave, and thank You that You left them there when You were resurrected.*
>
> *(If you have already been baptized, pray this:) Lord Jesus, I thank You that when I was baptized I was carried with You into Your death and resurrection. I will lay hold of the truth of Your Word that I am now a new creation, grafted into Your vine, and I am a child of God. Therefore, when the enemy tries to convince me to live like I did before, and he causes me to be tempted and struggle in the same sins as my ancestors, I can boldly point back to my baptism. I can decree that it is no longer I who live but Christ who lives in me. I am able to plead Jesus's blood over these things and sever them off my life. I ask You to give me the gift of the Holy Spirit in greater*

measure, that I would be led by You and empowered as I lay my life down at Your feet.

(If you have not been baptized, are unsure about the involvement of your own faith during baptism, or unsure about the validity of the ministry who performed your baptism, pray this:) Lord, thank You for what You did when You died for my sins and were raised from the dead. I believe that I have been carried with You into this by faith, not of my own works, but I want to show the world this faith and I want to experience being carried with You into laying my life down and receiving Your new life. I want to experience all that You have for me in baptism. Therefore, please help me find the right time, location, and ministry to assist me in being water-baptized. I am looking forward to the spiritual transformation that will happen in my own life.

Chapter 9

The Wonder of Being a New Creation and Ambassador of God

WHEN A PERSON TRULY receives Jesus as their Lord and Savior, it is a death to life miracle. In fact a series of miracles lead up to this change, and a series of miracles continue onward, though they may not be obviously apparent. Some people have amazing testimonies of spiritual realities colliding with and overflowing into the natural during their salvation experience. But often it is a quiet laying down of one's life in submission to God upon recognizing what Christ has done for them.

Recall from a few chapters ago, an aspect of faith is

believing even when we can't see. In salvation, we can't see our sins being covered by the blood of Christ and washed away, but the Word of God tells us this is true (1 John 1:7). Likewise, we can't necessarily see that we have been made new creations, but it is nevertheless true (2 Corinthians 5:17). So when you still feel dirty after genuine repentance, and it seems as though nothing has changed in you, what are you going to believe?

Historically, many theologians and denominations of Christianity have run into problems when they can't see certain Bible passages "working" in people's lives. They may assume these verses to be allegorical or merely poetic language. Some change their belief system and application of Scripture to align with ideas like "God doesn't do that anymore," "this applies only in spirit," or "that is reserved for Heaven." But we must know that the Word of God is not always automatic in its effects.

For example, God says to be holy as He is holy (1 Peter 1:13-16), and that we are the righteousness of God in Christ Jesus (2 Corinthians 5:21). But we find very soon after giving our lives to God that we still have sin crouching at the door, and experience will scream we are incapable of overcoming it. The new Christian still has lies they believe, and their perception may confirm it is utter truth. So should we change the verses above to fit our experience, or should we allow the Word to change us?

Oh, Lord, let us humble ourselves and be changed by Your Word!

God doesn't force us to be holy. And unless we join with Him in crucifying the flesh, sanctification, and discipline, Jesus's righteousness in us is going to be hidden by our carnality. So we aren't excused to think, *When God said be holy, He only meant when we get to heaven.*

When we weary of waiting on His promises, feel like we can't change, or the enemy tempts us into doubt and skepticism, we must go back to God's Word and declare that it *is* true no matter what our circumstances tell us. And we need to stir up a faith and zeal that says, "I am not giving up even if I die waiting for His promises (Hebrews 11:13-16)."

Many things change immediately and beautifully when we give our lives to Jesus. But probably more often than we would like (because it means we are responsible), we must join with God in receiving and applying His promises. We want God to do it all, and the enemy and religious people will tell you anything else is out of bounds. But the fact is, some Scriptures have to be fought for in faith, boldly proclaimed, even apprehended violently, and acted upon before they're manifestation is seen.

> *... the kingdom of heaven suffers violent assault, and violent men seize it by force [as a*

precious prize].
                    Matthew 11:12b AMP

Believe the Amazing and Life-Changing Truth that You Are a New Creation

"For the love of Christ compels us, because we judge thus: that if One died for all, then all died; and He died for all, that those who live should live no longer for themselves, but for Him who died for them and rose again. Therefore, from now on, we regard no one according to the flesh. Even though we have known Christ according to the flesh, yet now we know Him thus no longer. Therefore, if anyone is in Christ, he is a new creation; old things have passed away; behold, all things have become new. Now all things are of God, who has reconciled us to Himself through Jesus Christ, and has given us the ministry of reconciliation, that is, that God was in Christ reconciling the world to Himself, not imputing their trespasses to them, and has committed to us the word of reconciliation. Now then, we are ambassadors for Christ, as though God were

> *pleading through us: we implore you on Christ's behalf, be reconciled to God. For He made Him who knew no sin to be sin for us, that we might become the righteousness of God in Him."*
> II Corinthians 5:14-21 NKJV

There are so many times I come back to these verses and proclaim them. I must stand on them, because I don't always feel or act like I am a new creation in Christ. But this is what the Bible tells me I am. I have chosen to believe the Word of God over my feelings and experiences. And I can confirm that the more I have believed and acted on these verses, the more my feelings and experiences have followed the Word.

This passage applies to us in many ways. I encourage you to consider these truths the next time you are struggling, the next time the enemy is whispering lies in your ear about your identity, the next time God calls you to minister like Him. You are a new creation and an ambassador for Christ.

This truth and transformation will change your life and the lives of the people around you. It will cause you to represent God to the world, and appeal to others to turn their lives toward Him. As you do this, the Holy Spirit will flow through you, and you will see others transform into new creations in Christ.

Fullness of Joy

The Old Testament says we are fearfully and wonderfully made (Psalm 139:13-16). How much more awesome are we made new in Christ? This new creation experience is meant to bring life to your mortal body (Romans 8:11) and transformation in your soul (Romans 12:2). Possibly the most amazing miracle is that your spirit comes to life.

Often the Greek word translated as "spirit," in the New Testament is "pneúma (Strong's number 4151 in the Greek Lexicon[2])." Translators only determine which English word to use by the context, because pneúma can mean breath, wind, angels, demons, the Holy Spirit, and our spirit. As you are created new, the same substance that the Spirit of God is comes to life in you. As the wind of the Holy Spirit, which raised Christ from the dead, blows in and mixes with your spirit, you are then identified as a child of God (Romans 8:9-17).

When you consider this fact and how Jesus taught His disciples to follow in His footsteps, the potential in us starts to become clear—although the possibilities unimaginable. There are likely many reasons most Christians don't experience their potential as children of God. A lack of knowledge, false-humility, doubt and unbelief, carnality, selfish-gain, pride, and the spirit of religion (not to mention constantly thinking of ourselves as sinners and not much greater than worms).

But did you know your spirit is not held bound by the confines of your body? I'm not talking about astral projection, although that is real and not something we should pursue. There are many testimonies in Scripture about people being involved in supernatural feats in spirit and by the Holy Spirit. Just to name a few:

- Believers visiting heaven (2 Corinthians 12:1-4, Revelation 4:1-2)
- Prophets hearing enemies' plans (Jeremiah 11:18, 2 Kings 6:12)
- Philip moved supernaturally to another location (Acts 8:39-40)
- Paul visited churches in the spirit (Colossians 2:5)
- Jesus heard people's thoughts, disappeared in crowds, walked on water, and through walls (read the Gospels and look for this type of stuff!)
- Even now, your spirit is seated in heavenly places with Christ (Ephesians 2:6)

There are many modern-day testimonies of these things happening to missionaries and others in the body of Christ. But I believe it's possible for us to have even more of these types of experiences as we receive greater revelation, and an unlocking of who we are supposed to be in Christ. Can you imagine if even 10% of Christians started regularly

Fullness of Joy

doing these things?

What if the body of Christ actually acted like Jesus? Healing and setting people free easily, preaching to thousands with only their voice, multiplying food, and paying their taxes with long long-lost coins from the sea? All of this not for pride, or fun, or our own glory; but to bring glory to the Father, and that people would know Him and come to Him?

> *The entire universe is standing on tiptoe, yearning to see the unveiling of God's glorious sons and daughters!*
> Romans 8:19 TPT

The time has come for us to worship in spirit and in truth (John 4:23-24). All of creation is longing for these types of believers. You and I are two of them! When we rise up with the rest of God's new creation, will this not be a fulfillment of the knowledge of the glory of the Lord filling the earth as the waters cover the sea (Habakuk 2:14)?

Prayer

> *Father, thank You for making me a new creation and an ambassador of Your kingdom. I want to represent you well. Not to make a name for myself, but that the world would see*

You clearly. Right now I lay down all false-humility, doubt and unbelief, carnality, pride, selfish-gain, and weak religion. Please transform and expand my thinking. Please increase my faith. Please help me to boldly and zealously apprehend these promises. Thank You, Holy Spirit, for dwelling richly within me, making me a child of God, and helping me to be like Jesus.

Chapter 10

The Freedom that Comes from Laying Down Your Life

THE ENEMY HAS CONVINCED the world that freedom comes by doing whatever we want and a shedding of moral rules, leading to the deepest depravity. But as people participate in every kind of sin, their souls are bound, put into cages, blindfolded, gagged, abused, and become slaves. Whether or not this manifests obviously in life, doesn't make it any less true.

It is the saddest thing to watch someone, in the name of freedom, intentionally walk into the enemies' snares, thinking all that exists is what they can experience with

Fullness of Joy

their natural senses. Especially Christians who abuse the grace of God to live however they want, holding to verses about the depravity of man, and saying the verses about holiness are only in spirit and tied to the afterlife. These people are almost as bound as their heathen neighbors.

> *'I know your deeds, that you are neither cold nor hot; I wish that you were cold or hot. So because you are lukewarm, and neither hot nor cold, I will vomit you out of My mouth. Because you say, "I am rich, and have become wealthy, and have no need of anything," and you do not know that you are wretched, miserable, poor, blind, and naked, I advise you to buy from Me gold refined by fire so that you may become rich, and white garments so that you may clothe yourself and the shame of your nakedness will not be revealed; and eye salve to apply to your eyes so that you may see. Those whom I love, I rebuke and discipline; therefore be zealous and repent. Behold, I stand at the door and knock; if anyone hears My voice and opens the door, I will come in to him and will dine with him, and he with Me. The one who overcomes, I will grant to him to sit with Me on My throne, as I also overcame*

> *and sat with My Father on His throne.*
> Revelation 3:15-21 NASB

If we humble ourselves and allow Jesus to show us our need, we can have freedom. Not only that, but we can enter a deep fellowship with Him. It's when we take up our cross daily and follow Him, that the enemy loses his hooks in us.

When Jesus was telling His disciples that He was about to go to the Father, He said the enemy was coming to Him, but he had nothing in Him (John 14:30-31). Likewise, as you lay your life down at the feet of Jesus, you will begin to find that you are the freest person in the room. There are no hooks holding you to this world and keeping you from being who God created you to be.

True Freedom

It seems counterintuitive, but true freedom increases based on the amount you can become a slave of Christ. If you look at the introduction of several of Paul's letters in the Bible, you will see he joyfully introduced himself as a servant, bond-servant, slave, and prisoner of Christ (Philippians, Romans, Titus, and Philemon). As Paul laid down his life, while onlookers may have thought he was sacrificing treasures to God, he had a revelation:

> *I once thought these things were valuable, but*

Fullness of Joy

> *now I consider them worthless because of what Christ has done. Yes, everything else is worthless when compared with the infinite value of knowing Christ Jesus my Lord. For His sake I have discarded everything else, counting it all as garbage, so that I could gain Christ and become one with Him.*
> Philippians 3:7-9a NLT

I have seen in my own life, every time God asks me to give up something I think I want, He always has something much better in store for me. I am not saying this in pride or to gain approval from anyone, but I have given all my possessions, all my money, all my family and friends to Him, and He has proven faithful and more valuable every time.

He is not a mean father who takes away his children's toys as a power play. No, He loves His children and snatches them from the fire, bringing them into deep pleasures that are found at His right hand. Not everyone is called to give up everything, but no matter what He asks for, we can trust He is worth it.

Even if you give Him all your precious prizes, the people you love, and everything you value in this world, I promise what you gain in Christ far outweighs it all. Even your righteousness is as filthy rags according to Isaiah 64:6 and needs to be laid low. All your accomplishments and the religious boxes you have put God in, need to be placed on the altar and burned with holy fire.

As You Lay Down Your Life You Will Encounter Trials

As Jesus was continuing to prepare His disciples for His crucifixion, He told them that they would abandon Him, but He would still have the Father with Him. Then He said, "I have told you these things, so that in Me you may have [perfect] peace and confidence. In the world you have tribulation and trials and distress and frustration; but be of good cheer [take courage; be confident, certain, undaunted]! For I have overcome the world. [I have deprived it of power to harm you and have conquered it for you.] (John 16:33 AMPC)"

Following Jesus does not mean that everything goes perfectly. In fact, things can get very hard for you as the world understands you less and less, and the enemy strategizes against you more and more. In the midst of this, Jesus tells us to have perfect peace, confidence, and good cheer.

> *Therefore, since we have been made right in God's sight by faith, we have peace with God because of what Jesus Christ our Lord has done for us. Because of our faith, Christ has brought us into this place of undeserved*

> *privilege where we now stand, and we confidently and **joyfully** look forward to sharing God's glory.*
>
> *We can **rejoice**, too, when we run into problems and trials, for we know that they help us develop endurance. And endurance develops strength of character, and character strengthens our confident hope of salvation. And this hope will not lead to disappointment. For we know how dearly God loves us, because He has given us the Holy Spirit to fill our hearts with His love.*
>
> Romans 5:1-5 NLT (emphasis added, see also James 1:2-8)

Jesus said He has overcome the world, and we have promises that no weapon formed against us will prosper (Isaiah 54:17). This doesn't mean the weapons of the world and the enemy will not be forged, but that we do not need to fear them. James 1:2-8 also tells us we can count it all joy and allow every trial to increase our patience. And we have this promise that if we ask for wisdom with faith, God will give it to us liberally!

John W. Nichols

Not Really a Sacrifice but an Investment

> *And he who does not take his cross [expressing a willingness to endure whatever may come] and follow Me [believing in Me, conforming to My example in living and, if need be, suffering or perhaps dying because of faith in Me] is not worthy of Me. Whoever finds his life [in this world] will [eventually] lose it [through death], and whoever loses his life [in this world] for My sake will find it [that is, life with Me for all eternity].*
> Matthew 10:38-39 AMP

As I said in Chapter 1, it was for the *joy* that was set before Him that Jesus endured the cross (Hebrews 12:1-2). He was expecting God to work this out for good, and God had planned that act to be the turning point of mankind. The redemption of the whole world was purchased by Jesus's act of laying down His life.

Stop here, and instead of thinking about the sacrifice, think of how Jesus was giving something joyfully, knowing He would gain a return. Yes, it was costly, incomprehensibly so, but can you see the return on His investment?

Fullness of Joy

> *"Heaven's kingdom realm is also like a jewel merchant in search of rare pearls. When he discovered one very precious and exquisite pearl, he immediately gave up all he had in exchange for it."*
>
> Matthew 13:45-46 TPT

Just as Jesus said, unless a grain of wheat goes into the ground and dies there cannot be a harvest. Even so our lives or whatever we give to God as a sacrifice becomes a seed, and through it God makes life spring out of the dirt (John 12:23-26 paraphrased). The seed is valuable, but the farmer recognizes that each seed sown has the potential to produce many more seeds in the fruit. He thinks beyond the seed to reaping a bountiful harvest, not only in that season but for generations.

When you lay down your life you can also expect God to work it out for good. Please hear me that this is not a compromise, or a concession, or a thing lost. Recognize it is not really a sacrifice, or a sad thing, because what you are "giving up" doesn't compare to what you gain. Therefore, you can give in joy!

Prayer

Jesus, please help me to follow in Your footsteps of laying down my life, removing every hook the enemy has placed in me, letting go of all that weighs me down, and beginning to walk in the freedom and destiny that You have for me. Thank You, Jesus, for being my model and showing me how to follow our Heavenly Father despite the response of the enemy, the world, and even my closest friends. As I take up my cross and follow You, I ask You for perfect peace, courage, good cheer, patience, wisdom, and joy! And, Holy Spirit, I give You permission to show me anything that I need to lay down at the foot of the cross. I will do it joyfully, knowing I am purchasing this precious and exquisite pearl that is Your kingdom and fellowship with You. In Jesus's name, amen!

Chapter 11

What It Looks Like to Bear God's Fruit

I tell you the truth, unless a kernel of wheat is planted in the soil and dies, it remains alone. But its death will produce many new kernels—a plentiful harvest of new lives.

John 12:24 NLT

WE REFERENCED THESE WORDS of Jesus in the last chapter. Reaping a harvest of what is sown is a law of God's creation, both in the spiritual and natural realms. It effects every person and is not only true for believers and the idea of the gospel spreading. It is a truth that goes back to the garden, as God created things to reproduce after their own kind.

Fullness of Joy

> *Do not be deceived, God is not mocked; for whatever a man sows, that he will also reap. For he who sows to his flesh will of the flesh reap corruption, but he who sows to the Spirit will of the Spirit reap everlasting life. And let us not grow weary while doing good, for in due season we shall reap if we do not lose heart.*
> Galatians 6:7-9 NKJV

Just like you can't sow apple seeds and get corn in the harvest, it is a law that we will reap what we sow. People are gathering a harvest of what they have planted, even though they have no idea of this truth. And if you sow blessings, healing, love, compassion, and finances into God's kingdom, you can expect to receive a harvest of the same in your own life and ministry.

The Most Valuable Harvest

But the most valuable fruit you can bear is—the fruit of the Spirit. The way we reap this harvest is by investing in our relationship with the Holy Spirit and allowing Him to lead and change us (Galatians 5:16 and 18). This fruit is an outflowing of God's personality and goodness being expressed in everything we do. As the Spirit of God's life is born in us, a blessing will come upon every other thing we sow and reap.

> *But the fruit of the Spirit [the result of His presence within us] is love [unselfish concern for others], joy, [inner] peace, patience [not the ability to wait, but how we act while waiting], kindness, goodness, faithfulness, gentleness, self-control.*
> Galatians 5:22-23a AMP

The context of these verses shows the contrast of being led by the flesh and being led by the Holy Spirit. The law of sowing and reaping applies both to followers of Jesus, and those who don't even know He exists. Sometimes the Holy Spirit leads unbelievers, but for the most part they are led by their flesh and they reap what they unknowingly sow.

Because all people were created in God's image, every person is capable of a semblance and shadow of each of these fruit, no matter their faith. So of course people who are not born again can express a measure of love, joy, peace, patience, kindness, goodness, faithfulness, gentleness, and self-control. But when compared to the true fruit of the Spirit, the root is shallow and it withers away much quicker.

As a person gets connected to the One True God they start to taste and see His goodness that far surpasses the goodness of man. Then that goodness begins to manifest in their lives. As they submit themselves to His Holy Spirit, suddenly they find they're able to experience the fruit of the Spirit in a much richer, deeper, truer way than they ever tasted before.

The enemy would tell you that you can't bear this fruit, and you will always fail in these areas, but that's a lie. You are God's child. You are being transformed into His image from glory to glory. As you look at yourself in the mirror of God's word (James 1:22-27), and you see your weaknesses and changes needed, the grace of God abounds and strengthens you to do all things in Christ. Then the Holy Spirit will empower you to show the world what it looks like when a believer bears God's fruit.

Abundant Harvests in Everything We Sow

As we look at the Old Testament, we see that the people of God flourished. When they were obedient to God, they had blessings in every area. The fruit of their harvest was plentiful, even at times during drought. And when they didn't have harvests in the droughts, God provided supernaturally in other ways.

Check out this description of a righteous person from the Old Testament:

> *His pleasure and passion is remaining true to the Word of "I Am," meditating day and night*

> *in the true revelation of light. He will be standing firm like a flourishing tree planted by God's design, deeply rooted by the brooks of bliss, bearing fruit in every season of his life. He is never dry, never fainting, ever blessed, ever prosperous.*
> Psalms 1:2-3 TPT

The promises of the new covenant that we have with Christ are even better (Hebrews 8:6). We should be more blessed than people like Abraham in the Bible. There are so many promises in Scripture about blessing and provision, like the passage above in Psalm 1. We are meant to be planted by the stream of His living water, bearing fruit in every good work that we do. If we aren't getting that harvest, it may be that we need to proclaim God's Word, and command whatever is getting in the way to be changed.

It only makes sense that you would be blessed as you walk by the Spirit and bear His fruit of love, joy, peace, patience, kindness, goodness, faithfulness, gentleness, and self-control. You are going to have favor with God and with man. The Holy Spirit will lead you and give you wisdom, and you will represent Him well as you follow Him into the world and bring His kingdom.

You will find that you are not only harvesting blessings in this world, but you will naturally begin to invest in eternity. You will start to build treasures in heaven, instead of only building wealth on earth (which you can't bring with you when you die). You will also begin to sow into the harvest-field of souls, and your harvest will be eternal.

Before sending His disciples to preach the kingdom, Jesus told them, "The harvest truly is great, but the laborers are few; therefore pray the Lord of the harvest to send out laborers into His harvest (Luke 10:2 NLT)." When you get to heaven you won't have the opportunity to lead people to Jesus. This is your one chance, and you need to sow into it. You can pray into that harvest as well as offer yourself up to be sent.

The Personality of Jesus

The Holy Spirit is the person of God that the Father sent in a special way on the heels of Jesus's time on Earth. Where Jesus was *beside* His disciples as He led them, now His Spirit is leading from the *inside*. When Jesus told His disciples He was going away, He said:

> *"I will ask the Father, and He will give you **another** Comforter (Counselor, Helper, Intercessor, Advocate, Strengthener, and Standby), that He may remain with you*

forever—The Spirit of Truth..."
John 14:16-17a AMPC
(Emphasis added)

The reason Jesus said the Holy Spirit is "another," is because He is like Jesus. The Holy Spirit is Jesus *IN* you, leading you into truth, comforting, counseling, helping, interceding, advocating, strengthening, and standing by you—forever.

We are going to talk about the Holy Spirit and His gifts much more in later books in this series. Our focus for this chapter is His fruit. The fruit of the Spirit is Jesus's personality shining through you. Jesus's love springs up and pours out of you. His joy and peace and patience are like a river in your soul. As you go through life, you can tap into Jesus's divine kindness, goodness, faithfulness, gentleness, and self-control.

Every one of the fruit (His personality traits), are of utmost value. We could devote time to each, but this book is specifically about joy. Remember how we talked about Jesus being happy? His Spirit is joyful too. As you submit to the Holy Spirit, and allow Him to lead and change you, one of His characteristics that is going to bubble up and overflow out of you is joy!

Fullness of Joy

Prayer

Holy Spirit, I submit myself to you. I'm sorry for being led by my flesh and planting seeds that will not bring life to me and the people around me. Please help me to sow what will reap a harvest of blessings. Not only for prosperity and blessing in this world, but that I would store up treasures in heaven, including investing in souls. Please also search me and reveal any ways that I am not reflecting Jesus's personality in my life. Help me invest in our relationship, Holy Spirit, to be led by you and transformed to look and act like Jesus. Thank you, Lord. Amen!

Chapter 12

The Joy of Abiding in Christ

Spend Quality Time with Him

GOD IS A PERSON. We see this in so many ways through Scripture. He is described as seeing, hearing, reaching out, becoming angered and jealous, being gracious and merciful. Jesus too showed that He had compassion, wept, and loved in the Gospels. The Holy Spirit is grieved by sin, as well as how people keep Him from moving in other's lives.

One of the most amazing personality traits of God is His love for us as His children, and that He wants an intimate relationship with each of us. He desires for us to spend time with Him, be restored when we mess up, and tell Him all

Fullness of Joy

our hopes and dreams. He wants us to listen to Him and receive the instruction that only He can give. And those who seek Him find that He rewards them (Hebrews 11:6).

Working in church (and as a pastor for a span) I've heard many people asked how their quality time with Jesus is. Often the response goes something like, "I don't have time to stop and pray, so I just pray as I go." I understand this. There are seasons in our lives that are especially hard, or time consuming. But I wonder if these people found time to look at social media, play a game, or watch a show. Could they really not squeeze in at least fifteen minutes with the lover of their souls?

I have been guilty of this too, and so I am preaching to the choir. It's time we address this and call it what it is, so we can grow. We show our love, value, and appreciation by how we spend our time. We can and should pray as we go, but we also need to spend regular quality time with Jesus. It's not only the best way to spend our time, but it is the most fulfilling investment we can make.

If I never find time to get alone with my wife, look at her, listen to her, and talk with her without distractions, it is going to cause problems in our marriage. We could go through a period like this, and stay married, continue to be faithful, and love one another, but our relationship would suffer. The same is true with God.

So I encourage you to find a place and time to meet with

Jesus—every day. Yes, read your Bible. Yes, pray and ask Him for help, and thank Him for what He is doing in your life. But don't forget to wait on Him and give Him room to speak. No good relationship is one-sided, including your relationship with God.

Abide in Christ Everywhere You Go

> *"I am a true sprouting vine, and the farmer who tends the vine is my Father. He cares for the branches connected to me by lifting and propping up the fruitless branches and pruning every fruitful branch to yield a greater harvest. The words I have spoken over you have already cleansed you. So you must remain in life-union with me, for I remain in life-union with you. For as a branch severed from the vine will not bear fruit, so your life will be fruitless unless you live your life intimately joined to mine.*
>
> *"I am the sprouting vine queen and you're my branches. As you live in union with me as your source, fruitfulness will stream from within you—but when you live separated from me you are powerless. If a person is separated from*

Fullness of Joy

> *me, he is discarded; such branches are gathered up and thrown into the fire to be burned. But if you live in life-union with me and if my words live powerfully within you—then you can ask whatever you desire and it will be done. When your lives bear abundant fruit, you demonstrate that you are my mature disciples who glorify my Father!*
>
> *"I love each of you with the same love that the Father loves me. You must continually let my love nourish your hearts. If you keep my commands, you will live in my love, just as I have kept my Father's commands, for I continually live nourished and empowered by his love. My purpose for telling you these things is so that the joy that I experience will fill your hearts with overflowing gladness!*
>
> John 15:1-11 TPT (read also 12-17)

This is a picture of what happened to you when you gave your life to Jesus. Where The Passion Translation says to live in "life-union," other translations use the word "abide." Abiding in Christ means to remain connected to the life-giving vine that is Jesus, wherever you go and whatever you are doing. When you do this, your life will bear much fruit.

Unfortunately, when many Christians step out of church

or their prayer closet, they leave Jesus there. We are not meant to just go through our days and do whatever we want acting as if God is not with us. This is almost as bad as the foolish unbeliever who says there is no God (Psalms 14). We need to remember that He is always with us, and we need to act like this is true all day, every day.

A farmer can cut a branch off one tree, and splice it onto another tree. The farmer cuts the branches so they will fit, and he binds them together. The two branches then heal, become one, and continue to grow. Then the roots are able to supply the needs of the branch from the other tree. And the branch that was cut from its original trunk is even capable of bearing fruit.

In the same way, God wants us always connected to Jesus. We have been severed from our old life and grafted in to Jesus's life. How can we bear fruit if we act as if we are not connected to the vine? In the verses above, God says He will cut these types of branches off and throw them in the fire. So, we need to abide, living in habitual union with Christ. Staying near to Him, remembering that He is always with us, and allowing Him to work in and through us.

Fullness of Joy

Joy Is Found through Connecting with Jesus

At the end of that passage, we read the reason Jesus was telling us this:

> *"These things I have spoken to you, that My **joy** may remain in you, and that your **joy** may be full."*
> John 15:11 NKJV (emphasis added)

The fullness of joy is experienced as you:

- allow your Heavenly Father to prune you with His loving discipline
- connect with Jesus and receive His life-source flowing through you
- remain in Him, never leaving Him or thinking you can do things on your own
- listen to Him, letting His words live in you, and asking what you desire
- bear His fruit as His disciple who glorifies the Father
- keep Jesus's commandments and follow Him
- receive and express the love His Father gave Him, and that He shares with you.

Partnering with the Holy Spirit in these things, will

cause Jesus's joy to remain in you, and allow your joy to be full. Did you get that? Full! This is the key to experiencing the *fullness* of joy.

Compassion Flows through the Vine

> *Jesus was going through all the cities and villages, teaching in their synagogues and proclaiming the gospel of the kingdom, and healing every disease and every sickness. Seeing the crowds, He felt compassion for them, because they were distressed and downcast, like sheep without a shepherd.*
> Matthew 9:35-36 NASB

I love this passage that shows Jesus's heart for the people. There are many places in Scripture where it says Jesus was moved with compassion as He ministered. When you are connected to the vine, the love of God is able to flow through you. As this happens you will care so deeply and truly want the best for people around you—just as Jesus did.

There have been a few times where my wife and I felt this powerful, supernatural compassion of the Lord come upon us during ministry. We felt so much love for the people that we were ministering to. It was like they were our best friends even though we barely knew them and sometimes didn't know them at all. What God did during those times was amazing!

Even if you are not "in ministry" you will be able to minister in that love and compassion of the Father's heart as you abide in Christ. Whether at your workplace, or home, or the church, the gym, or the park, your ministry will be extremely effective. The power of God is going to flow through you freely without inhibitions, and hearts will be transformed.

Like Jesus saw what His Father was doing and He joined in. You will go through your days looking around you and seeing what God is up to. You will know that clerk at the grocery store needs to hear how Jesus loves them. You will have supernatural faith to lay hands and command that co-worker to be healed. You will have profound wisdom as you prophesy to your friend who is going through a hard season in life.

This is how you and others like you will represent the Kingdom of God on the earth. And you will inspire other Christians to listen in faith and boldly obey the Holy Spirit. As the Body of Christ takes up this opportunity and responsibility, the glory of God will be made manifest and cover the earth, as the waters cover the sea. This is the inheritance of the children of God.

John W. Nichols

Prayer

Jesus, I want to live in connection with You and always recognize that You are with me. Thank You for grafting me into Your life-giving vine, giving me Your Holy Spirit to abide in me, and calling me to remain in You. Thank You, that as I abide in You, I will bear much fruit and I will experience your love and fullness of joy. Just as You were moved with compassion, Jesus, I ask that I would be led by the Father and minister to the people around me in His great love.

*Oh Lord, as we end this book I pray that I would be like Paul who said, "To me, who am less than the least of all the saints, this grace was given, **that I should preach** among the Gentiles **the unsearchable riches of Christ**, and to **make all see what is the fellowship of the mystery, which from the beginning of the ages has been hidden in God who created all things through Jesus Christ**; to the intent that now **the manifold wisdom of God might be made known by the church** to the principalities and powers in the heavenly places, according to the eternal purpose which*

Fullness of Joy

*He accomplished in Christ Jesus our Lord, in whom **we have boldness and access with confidence through faith in Him**..."*

*For this reason I bow my knees to the Father of our Lord Jesus Christ, from whom the whole family in heaven and earth is named, that **He would grant [us], according to the riches of His glory, to be strengthened with might through His Spirit in the inner man**, that Christ may dwell in [our] hearts through faith; that [we], being rooted and grounded in love, may be able to comprehend with all the saints what is the width and length and depth and height— to know the love of Christ which passes knowledge; that [we] **may be filled with all the fullness of God**."*

*Now to Him who is able to do exceedingly abundantly above all that we ask or think, according to **the power that works in us**, to Him be glory in the church by Christ Jesus to all generations, forever and ever. Amen (Ephesians 3:8-12; 14-21 emphasis added)."*

Additional Notes

I HOPE MY WORDS have blessed you and encouraged you to step into the calling you have in Christ. If they have, there are a few ways you can be even more blessed, forward the blessing to someone else, and help me at the same time. Check out all the free stuff I have for you below and find out how to partner with me and my family.

Who Needs to Hear this Message?

Take a moment and ask God to show you who else this book could help. He may bring someone to your mind that you want to be inspired to change the world. Or maybe someone who needs a dose of joy, or a deeper revelation of salvation. This book and the following books in the series would also be good for Bible study material.

If you or someone you know is fighting for physical healing or would like to learn more about how to pray for healing, you should check out my book, *Healing is Here*. It is a 7-week devotional that shows God's will to heal and how to pray for it using Biblical examples. Find out more at:

Fullness of Joy

GodAndYouAndMe.com/Healing-is-Here-Book

If you know someone who is going through a hard time, or struggling with questions about life and God, you can let them know they can get my ebook *GOD is HERE*, the accompanying workbook and journal, audiobook, and PDF on salvation and the gift of the Holy Spirit for free here:

GodAndYouAndMe.com/God-is-Here-Free-Stuff

Reviews are a Huge Help to Authors

Another way to help is with a few minutes of your time by leaving a quick review wherever you got this book. Reviews really help people to know if they should check out a book. You can review it on Amazon, Good Reads, Barnes & Noble, iBooks, Kobo, and/or Google Play Books. Please take a couple of minutes to review this book on one or more of these sites. I appreciate your feedback, so I can learn to communicate God's heart better, and hopefully reach more people. Thank you in advance!

More Free Books!

If you're interested in being an advance reader and have the opportunity to get future books for free, visit:

GodAndYouAndMe.com/Advance-Reader

Updates and Partnering with My Family

If you'd like an update on what God is doing with me and my family, and would like to support us in prayer or financially visit:

GodAndYouAndMe.com/Ministry-Partner

My Contact Information

Check out the About the Author chapter below for a bit more info about me and my family, as well as how you can contact me, connect on social media, and receive encouraging blog posts on my website. I would love to hear any testimonies of the work that God has done in your life through my work. Please reach out below.

Free Stuff!

IF YOU HAVEN'T ALREADY, you can download the free accompanying workbook to view on your phone/tablet or as a printable PDF. It will help you think deeper about these topics and apply the Biblical truths, especially if you step out in faith and follow the recommended Action Items. I created it as another tool for you to become a Holy Spirit-led, manifest child of God, who ignites unstoppable, joyful, revival fires of supernatural power!

In the download, I'll also include these other free resources that you can take advantage of!

Fullness of Joy Workbook   Simple Steps to Hearing God   Walk with God, Change the World   Revolutionize Your Quiet Time

Subscribe at: GodAndYouAndMe.com/joy-free-stuff

Fullness of Joy

Get All These Free Resources Together

- Printable PDF of the *Fullness of Joy that Only Comes with Salvation Workbook*. (also viewable on phone/tablet).
- *God is Trying to Tell You Something*. An audio teaching in MP3 format, focused on the key to hearing God, common ways God speaks, and practical steps to hear Him today.
- *7 Keys to a Successful Time of Devotion to God*. A PDF with steps to include in your quiet time.
- *Navigating the Maze of Life with God*. A 60-page PDF about giving your life to God, being filled with the Holy Spirit, and walking in the power of the Holy Spirit to live the life God intended you to live.
- Additional content only available to subscribers on GodAndYouAndMe.com. You can unsubscribe at any time and I promise not to spam you.

Get these free resources here (Most phones are capable of using the camera app to follow this link. Simply open the camera on your phone and point it at the page):

GodAndYouAndMe.com/joy-free-stuff

References

1. "4982. sózó." *biblehub.com.* Bible Hub, 2024. Web. 5 Jan. 2024.
   https://biblehub.com/greek/4982.htm.
2. "4151. pneúma." *biblehub.com.* Bible Hub, 2024. Web. 5 Jan. 2024.
   https://biblehub.com/greek/4151.htm.

About the Author

AT THE MENTION OF books John W. Nichols ears perk up, he gets a spine-tingling sensation (no pun intended), and he can't help but find out what read is on discussion. With his first computer at twelve years of age, John began writing, and he is an avid reader, always with a stack of books by his bedside and listening to as many audiobooks as possible when working on mindless tasks. When Jesus saved him at the age of twenty, John started reading the best book you could ever read, over and over, recognizing the Holy Bible as a letter from the Creator of all things.

He thought one day (when he was old) he might write a book for God. But God thought he should write something sooner, and told John in a prayer session on January 1st, 2016, to write his book. Since then, John has written four books including the one you are reading.

In other prayer sessions, God called John to preach His Word, seek His face, and go into the land He would show Him. He and his wife, Trinna, and three children, are

Fullness of Joy

following this call to show the love of Christ to the world. This was first exhibited teaching and leading worship in their local church, then by working with people with disabilities, then going to preach at the state prison, loving their neighborhood community, reaching out to women and children enslaved in human trafficking, and making disciples of Jesus who will multiply, and now serving as missionaries in Rome, Italy.

When John caught a glimpse of how God saw him, everything changed, and he has since sought to show others this good news. He's recognized most people, Christian or not, feel unfulfilled and don't know their life's purpose. This has led John to help people find their calling and have a life of adventure with God. To be encouraged in the way God sees you, and to keep up with what God is doing with John and his family, go to:

You can also connect with John in the following ways.
Email:
John@GodAndYouAndMe.com
Short words of encouragement:
GodAndYouAndMe.com/Blog

Social Media:
Facebook.com/GodAndYouAndMeBlog
YouTube.com/channel/UCqG-TKZgn2PwwEQx9WlThoA
Istagram.com/Nichols_JohnW
Twitter.com/Nichols_JohnW
Linkedin.com/in/GodAndYouAndMe
GoodReads.com/author/show/18325435.John_W_Nichols
Amazon.com/author/Nichols_JohnW

www.ingramcontent.com/pod-product-compliance
Lightning Source LLC
Chambersburg PA
CBHW060613080526
44585CB00013B/801